SIX

Ingredients
or Less®

Families
on the Go™

Also by Carlean Johnson

Six Ingredients or Less Cookbook

Six Ingredients or Less Chicken Cookbook

Six Ingredients or Less Cooking Light & Healthy

Six Ingredients or Less Pasta & Casseroles

Six Ingredients or Less Slow Cooker Cookbook

Six Ingredients or Less Low-Carb Cookbook

Six Ingredients or Less Diabetic Cookbook

(See page 286 for more information)

SIX

Ingredients
or Less®

Families
on the Go™

Carlean Johnson

CJ
BOOKS
Washington

Six Ingredients or Less®

Families on the Go™

Cover Design by Tanya Unger at Honeybee Promotions
Book design and production by Linda Hazen

Library of Congress Control Number: 2005906138
ISBN: 978-0-942878-09-7

CJ Books
PO Box 922
Gig Harbor, WA 98335
1-800-423-7184
sixingredientsorless.com
carlean@sixingredientsorless.com

Dedication

This book is dedicated to my daughter Linda, whose family is on-the-go, yet she makes it a priority for them to share dinner together. And to all "Families on the Go," who lead such busy lives, yet still strive to do what's best for their family - including preparing homecooked meals as often as possible.

Acknowledgements

Once again we have a new cookbook made possible only by the great team we have assembled. A heartfelt thanks just doesn't seem to be enough for all of the hard work involved.

First of all, I would like to thank my daughter, Linda Hazen, who once again is working with me after taking some time off to be with her family and to build their new house. I couldn't have a more dedicated and reliable person. I am truly thankful for all your hard work and for sharing your beautiful new kitchen with me.

I also want to thank Darlene Lindmark for all the long hours proofreading. This is now your third cookbook and you have become quite a pro. Thank you for doing such a good job.

A big thank you goes to my family and friends for being so patient with me when a new cookbook seems to consume most of my time.

Table of Contents

Ingredient List

Baked Pizza Crust   We used 14-inch Boboli®.

Baking Mix   We used Bisquick®.

Butter   In some recipes, margarine can be substituted for the butter, but bear in mind that margarine often contains water which may affect some recipes.

Eggs   Eggs are large size.

Flour   Measure by first stirring the flour so it is less compact, then lightly spoon into measuring cup before leveling off.

Measuring Cups   Use liquid measuring cups for all liquids and dry measuring cups for all dry ingredients.

Oils   We used Extra Light olive oil because of its versatility. It can be used for sauteing, salads, baking, etc.

Process Cheese Spread   American or Velveeta® cheese.

Vegetable Cooking Spray   Such as Pam®. Use when a recipe calls for a "sprayed" baking dish, baking pan or muffin tin.

Servings   Means servings, not necessarily people it will serve.

Introduction

Even with today's busy lifestyles, gathering your family around the table doesn't have to be a thing of the past. Just a little bit of planning and you can feed your family heart-warming comfort foods in less time than you might think. By planning your meals, shopping and having the ingredients on hand when you need them, your family will eat more delicious nutritious meals and you won't have a problem getting them to the table on time. In fact, once they get a whiff of what's cooking in the kitchen you may have all kinds of help wanting to get dinner on the table fast.

So, enjoy the comfort of gathering your family around the table more often, learn about their day, and share the pleasures of your day with them.

Happy Cooking!

Carlean

About the Author

Carlean's love of cooking has inspired her to write a series of popular cookbooks called Six Ingredients or Less. The new Families on the Go cookbook is the latest in her series. Carlean resides in Gig Harbor, Washington.

Appetizers & Beverages

Apricot Almond Brie

1	(8 to 10-oz) wedge Brie cheese
½	cup apricot preserves
1	tablespoon Grand Marnier liqueur
1	tablespoon toasted sliced almonds

Remove top rind from cheese. Place cheese on serving plate. In a small saucepan, combine preserves and liqueur and heat through, but do not boil.

Spoon some of the sauce over cheese (save remainder for later). Sprinkle almonds over top. Serve with butter crackers.

Stove Top

Probably my favorite appetizer, and definitely the one I use most often. Serve with a glass of white wine and your guests will never know it took you less than 10 minutes to put together.

Hot Artichoke Dip

1	(9-oz) can artichoke hearts, drained, coarsely chopped
1	(4-oz) can chopped green chilies
1	cup mayonnaise
1	cup grated Parmesan cheese

Combine ingredients in medium saucepan; heat through. Serve warm with chips, crackers, or bread cubes.

Stove Top

Variation: Add ½ cup smoked salmon, crab, bacon, or chopped water chestnuts. This is a 4th of July must for our family and friends.

Dill Dip

Chill

An oldie, but still a favorite. Serve with chilled fresh vegetables such as carrot sticks, cherry tomatoes, raw cauliflower, celery, cucumber rounds, and green pepper.

⅔	cup mayonnaise
⅔	cup sour cream
1	teaspoon dry minced onion
1	teaspoon dill weed
1	teaspoon Beau Monde seasoning

Combine ingredients until well mixed. Cover and chill several hours or overnight to blend flavors. Remove from refrigerator just prior to serving. Makes 1⅓ cups.

Heavenly Fruit Dip

Chill

It takes about 3 minutes to mix this and have it chilling in the refrigerator. Serve as a dip with fresh fruit or as a dressing over fruit salad. Yum!

1	(3.4-oz) box instant vanilla pudding mix
2½	cups Half and Half
1	tablespoon sugar
½	teaspoon rum extract
½	teaspoon vanilla extract

Combine ingredients in small mixing bowl; beat with rotary beater or lowest speed of mixer for about 2 minutes. Cover and chill several hours or overnight. Makes about 3 cups.

Peppered Cheese Dip

Microwave

Just heat the cheese and serve with bread cubes, chips, broccoli florets, cauliflower or cooked new potatoes.

Shredded Pepper Jack cheese, desired amount

Place cheese in a mound in center of a 9-inch pie dish. Microwave until melted, but not too runny.

Quick Bean Dip Nachos

Oven 350°F

1	bag round flat tortilla chips
1	(10½-oz) jar jalapeños bean dip
	Shredded Cheddar cheese

Spoon about a teaspoon of bean dip on center of each tortilla chip. Cover with a sprinkle of cheese. Place in a shallow baking pan and bake just long enough to melt the cheese. Serve hot.

If desired, these can be heated in the microwave.

Tip: Do not prepare ahead; the bean dip tends to soften the chips and make them tough and soggy.

Stuffed Pepper Shells

Oven 375°F

4	small red peppers, halved, seeded
1	cup (4-oz) Mozzarella cheese, shredded
2	tablespoons pesto

Fill peppers with cheese, mounding slightly. Place on a baking sheet and drizzle with pesto. Bake 10 to 12 minutes to melt the cheese. Serve hot.

A wonderful addition to a vegetable tray.

Appetizers

Serving a variety of appetizers will make for great conversation and more mingling among your guests. Keep it rather simple and do as much ahead as possible. After all, you want to enjoy the party too.

Baked Camembert

1   (8-oz) box Camembert

Remove cheese from box and unwrap. Return to box and cover. Remove all labels and place on baking sheet. Bake 25 to 30 minutes or until cheese is soft.

Carefully remove the top rind keeping cheese in the box. Serve with assorted veggies and crackers.

Oven 350°F

Tip: When serving a variety of appetizers, present a nice mixture of hot and cold.

Sausage Stuffed Mushrooms

Large mushrooms
Italian sausage
Grated Parmesan cheese

Wash mushrooms and remove stems and center, making room for the sausage.

Fill each mushroom with sausage until mounded and rather compact. Place on baking sheet and sprinkle lightly with Parmesan cheese. Bake 25 to 30 minutes or until sausage is cooked through. Serve hot.

Oven 350°F

Note: Allow 2 to 3 mushrooms per person.

Cream Cheese & Toppings

1   (8-oz) package cream cheese
     Assorted Toppings:

     Green Pepper Jelly
     Chutney
     Salsa
     Shrimp or crab in cocktail sauce
     Cranberry relish (check grocer's deli)
     Cranberry sauce

𝒫lace the cream cheese on a serving dish and top with desired topping. Serve with assorted crackers.

The mild flavor of table water crackers goes well with this recipe.

Quick Sweet & Sour Meatballs

Combine purchased precooked meatballs and purchased sweet-sour sauce in a saucepan or slow cooker. Heat through and serve with wooden picks. For additional flavor, add canned pineapple chunks, drained.

Appetizer Menu

Apricot Almond Brie

Hot Artichoke Dip

Dill Dip

Teriyaki Chicken Wings

Teriyaki Chicken Wings

Oven 350°F

A richly glazed appetizer that can also be served as a main dish. To make life even easier, I like to marinate meat and poultry in a large zip-type bag. This way, you simply flip the bag over a few times instead of having to turn each piece.

16	chicken drumettes (meaty leg portion)
¼	cup light soy sauce
¾	cup firmly packed brown sugar
1	tablespoon honey
4	thin slices fresh ginger
1	green onions, cut into 1-inch pieces

Rinse drumettes and pat dry. In a medium bowl, combine remaining ingredients, stirring to dissolve the sugar. Add chicken; cover and chill at least 3 hours, turning occasionally.

Place chicken, in one layer, on a foil-lined shallow baking pan. Bake 30 to 35 minutes, or until cooked through, basting frequently. Makes 8 servings of 2 each.

Little Tomatoes with Cheese

Oven 350°F

These are those beautiful little tomatoes that are still attached to the vine.

1	small red tomato, about 1½-inches
1	tablespoon Pepper Jack cheese, shredded
½	teaspoon sliced almonds, coarsely crumbled
	Chopped parsley

Remove a ¼-inch slice from the rounded part of the tomatoes (opposite the stem). Remove pulp and place up-side-down on paper towels to drain.

Form cheese into a sort of ball and fill tomato. There should be a slight mound above the tomato. Sprinkle with almonds and parsley. Bake 5 minutes to melt cheese. Don't overcook or the tomatoes will be too soft.

Easy Salsa

3	cups chopped Plum tomatoes
¼	cup chopped onion
1	(4-oz) can chopped green chilies
1	tablespoon apple cider vinegar
¾	teaspoon salt

Combine ingredients; cover and chill several hours to blend flavors. Makes about 3½ cups.

Chill

Serve as a dip or as a topping for meats, salads, and hamburgers.

Pineapple–Strawberry Fruit Salsa

1	(8-oz) can pineapple tidbits or ¾ cup
¾	cup chopped fresh strawberries
2	tablespoons finely chopped green pepper
1	tablespoon fresh lime juice
1	tablespoon apricot preserves

Combine ingredients; cover and chill until ready to serve. Makes 1¾ cups.

Chill

First we had tomato based salsas. Then we started adding corn, black beans and olives. Now we have fruit based salsas which are wonderful served with flank steak, chicken, turkey, ham or tortillas.

Corn–Tomato Salsa

1	cup fresh or frozen corn
1	cup chopped tomatoes (seeds removed)
¼	cup sliced green onions
1	small fresh jalapeño pepper, seeded and finely chopped
1	tablespoon chopped cilantro
1	tablespoon white wine vinegar

In a medium bowl, combine all the ingredients. Cover and chill until ready to serve. Makes 2¼ cups.

Chill

This salsa has a tasty southwestern kick to it.

Tortilla Appetizers

Chill

A nice make-ahead appetizer.

2	(8-oz) packages cream cheese
1	(1-oz) package Ranch dressing mix
¼	cup chopped green onions
½	cup finely chopped red peppers
½	cup chopped black olives
4	(10-inch) tortillas

Beat cream cheese until light. Add dressing mix and beat until blended. Add remaining ingredients and spread on the tortillas. Roll up tightly and wrap in wax paper, twisting ends. Chill at least 2 hours. Cut into 1-inch slices. Makes 40 appetizers.

Herbed Tomato Crostini

Oven 350°F

Crostinis have become very popular during the last few years. Serve with your favorite cold drink or as an accompaniment to salad or soup.

1	French bread baguette
¼	cup herb or other flavored olive oil
½	teaspoon minced fresh garlic
18	thin slices Mozzarella cheese (to fit bread)
4	medium Plum tomatoes, thinly sliced
	Chopped parsley or fresh basil leaves

Cut bread diagonally into ½-inch slices; place on a baking sheet. Combine oil and garlic. Brush on bread slices. Bake 6 to 8 minutes or until lightly toasted.

Top each with a slice of cheese and tomato. Lightly brush with remaining oil. Sprinkle with parsley or basil. Return to oven for just a minute to slightly soften the cheese. Makes 18 appetizers.

Sun Tea

1 gallon cold water
7 tea bags

Fill a gallon glass jar with water. Add tea bags; put lid on. Place outside in sun and leave several hours or until desired strength is achieved.

Note: This tea is mild with no hint of bitterness. Which means - you add less sugar. The water temperature determines the bitterness of the tea. The hotter the water - the more bitter the tea. The cooler the water - the less bitter the tea. Of course the colder water will take longer to brew, but it is worth it.

Variation: Add one to two tea bags of flavored tea. Two bags of peach, one of peppermint and 4 regular is a great combination.

White Grape Juice Spritzer

Chill

Per Drink:
  ¾ **cup white grape juice, chilled**
  ¾ **cup lemon-lime soda pop, chilled**
      Lime slices, cut in half

Combine ingredients. Pour into an attractive serving glass with ice. Add a lime slice and serve. Makes 1 serving.

This delicious nonalcoholic drink can be served with appetizers or as a beverage before dinner. It can also be made in a pitcher using equal quantities or to taste.

Easy Party Punch

Chill

Kind to your budget. Great for picnics, weddings, showers, parties, etc.

1	(.14-oz) package cherry Kool-Aid®
1	(.14-oz) package raspberry Kool-Aid®
2	cups sugar
2	quarts water
1	(46-oz) can unsweetened pineapple juice
2	quarts ginger ale (or to taste)

Combine first 5 ingredients, chill.

When ready to serve, stir in ginger ale. Makes 50 punch cup servings.

Sherbet Punch

This recipe makes a colorful punch for weddings, showers, Christmas or any special occasion. For a white wedding punch use vanilla ice cream.

2	quarts lime or raspberry sherbet
3	quarts lemon-lime soda pop, chilled

Spoon sherbet into a large punch bowl; pour in pop to taste. Stir carefully until most of the sherbet has dissolved. Makes 36 punch cup servings.

Holiday Eggnog Punch

This is a large recipe that will serve at least 12 to 14 people. If you have a small group, make half the recipe. The punch doesn't keep—so enjoy!

2	quarts purchased eggnog
1	quart vanilla ice cream, softened
1	(2-liter) bottle lemon-lime soda pop, chilled

Combine eggnog and ice cream in a large punch bowl. Gently stir in the pop. Makes about 4 quarts.

Paulina's Italian Cream Soda

2	tablespoons strawberry syrup, or to taste
1	cup chilled club soda
1	tablespoon heavy cream

Pour syrup into a glass filled with ice cubes. Add club soda. Stir in the cream.

If desired, garnish with a dollop of whipped cream and a strawberry slice.

Lime Spritzer

½	cup white wine
1	lime (1 tablespoon juice and 1 slice)
½	cup lemon-lime soda, or to taste

Combine wine, lime juice, and soda. Pour over ice. Garnish with a lime slice.

Good Wine Choices:

Chardonnay, Chablis, Riesling, etc.

Linda's Orange Julius

1	(6-oz) can frozen orange juice concentrate
1	teaspoon vanilla extract
1	cup milk
1	cup water
½	cup sugar
6	ice cubes

Place ingredients in blender and blend until thoroughly mixed and ice is crushed. Serve right away. Makes 3 to 4 servings.

Blender

Let the kids make this recipe for their next sleep-over.

Vanilla–Raspberry Treat

½   cup vanilla ice cream
½   cup diet or regular raspberry soda, chilled

Place ice cream in a 12-oz glass and pour raspberry soda over top. Makes 1 serving.

If desired, top with whipped cream or chocolate sprinkles.

Iced Latté

Chill

4   cups strong coffee
1   cup whipping cream
1   tablespoon sugar, or to taste

Combine ingredients and chill. Serve over ice.

For a more flavorful drink, you need to use strong brewed coffee.

Mochalicious

Delicious!
The taste testers loved this one.

½   cup whipping cream
2   teaspoons sugar, or to taste
1   teaspoon vanilla
½   ounce dark chocolate, grated
2   cups hot coffee

Combine whipping cream, sugar, and vanilla and beat until soft peaks form. Fold in chocolate.

Pour coffee into 2 coffee cups. Top with whipping cream. Makes 2 servings.

Breads

Easy Dinner Rolls

1	(8½-oz) box yellow or white cake mix
1	package dry yeast
½	teaspoon salt
1¼	cups hot tap water
2½	to 3 cups flour

Combine cake mix, yeast, and salt in a large bowl. Add water and flour to make a soft dough. (Dough will be quite sticky.) Cover; let rise until doubled, 1 to 1½ hours.

Stir down dough; spoon onto a well floured surface. Gently turn dough a couple of times to lightly coat with flour. Shape into desired size rolls and place on sprayed baking sheets. Or shape into balls and place in sprayed muffin tins. Cover and let rise until double, about 1 hour. Bake 10 to 15 minutes or until golden. Makes 15 to 18 rolls.

Oven 400°F

My mother told me about this recipe. Different, delicious, and very easy to prepare. My daughter likes to add 1½ teaspoons fresh orange peel for a delicious citrus flavor.

Quick Focaccia Bread

1	(10-oz) can refrigerated breadsticks
1	teaspoon olive oil
½	teaspoon basil
½	teaspoon rosemary
½	teaspoon garlic powder

Separate bread sticks, but do not unroll. Place on a sprayed baking sheet and press into 4-inch circles. Brush lightly with olive oil. Combine remaining ingredients; sprinkle over dough. Bake 12 to 15 minutes or until lightly browned. Makes 8 servings.

Oven 350°F

A nice crisp bread to serve with soups or salads.

This bread packs an impressive amount of flavor. Serve with barbecued ribs or grilled chicken. Add potato salad and corn on the cob and you have a full meal everyone will enjoy.

Herb Cheese Bread

1	loaf French bread, halved lengthwise
⅓	cup olive oil
½	teaspoon dried oregano, crushed
2	teaspoons dried basil, crushed
1	cup (4-oz) Monterey Jack cheese, shredded
1	cup (4-oz) Cheddar cheese, shredded

Combine oil, oregano, and basil. Spread on cut sides of bread. Combine cheese and sprinkle on bottom half of bread, using all the cheese. Top with second half of bread. Press slightly, making sure all of the cheese is inside the bread. Wrap in foil. Bake 10 to 15 minutes or until hot. Cut into 1½-inch slices. Makes 10 to 12 servings.

Oven 350°F

Tip: If a softer bread is desired, wrap in foil and then bake.

Garlic Bread

1	loaf French bread
½	cup butter, softened
1	to 2 small garlic cloves, minced

Cut bread in slices or cut in half lengthwise. Place on baking sheet. Combine butter and garlic, mixing well. Spread evenly on bread. Bake 8 to 10 minutes or until lightly toasted. Makes 10 to 12 servings.

Mincing Fresh Garlic

Here's an easy way: Place a garlic clove on a cutting board. Place the wide part of a chef's knife flat on the clove. Pound lightly to crush. Peel away the skin and finely chop.

Supper Cheese Bread

Oven 400°F

1½   cups baking mix
1   large egg
¼   cup milk
1   cup (4-oz) Cheddar cheese, shredded, divided
1   teaspoon poppy seeds
2   tablespoons butter, melted

A definite cheese flavor. Best served fresh from the oven, but can be reheated.

Combine baking mix, egg, milk, and ½ cup of the cheese; stir just until moistened. The dough will be stiff, but sticky. Pat dough evenly onto bottom of a sprayed 9-inch pie pan. Sprinkle with remaining cheese and poppy seeds; pour butter over top. Bake 20 to 25 minutes or until lightly browned. Cut into wedges and serve hot. Makes 6 servings.

Tomato-Garlic Pizza Bread

Oven 425°F

1   (13.6-oz) can refrigerated pizza crust
2   small garlic cloves, minced
¼   teaspoon dried oregano
1   cup (4-oz) Mozzarella cheese
2   Plum tomatoes, chopped

Variation: Omit tomatoes and top with assorted cheese such as Swiss, Mozzarella, Cheddar, or Gorgonzola. Add a little chopped onion, oregano, and freshly ground black pepper.

On a sprayed baking sheet, pat dough into about a 12x8-inch rectangle.

Sprinkle with garlic, oregano, and then the cheese. Top with chopped tomato. Bake 10 to 12 minutes or until crust is golden and cheese has melted. Makes 6 to 8 servings.

Cheesy Quick Bread

1	(13.6-oz) can refrigerated pizza crust
1	tablespoon olive oil
2	cups (8-oz) Mozzarella cheese, shredded
	Garlic salt
	Fresh or dried cilantro or parsley

On a sprayed baking pan or sheet, pat or roll pizza crust into a 12x8-inch rectangle. Brush with olive oil.

Sprinkle cheese evenly over crust. Sprinkle lightly with garlic salt and herbs. Bake 12 to 16 minutes or until crust is lightly browned. Makes 6 to 8 servings.

Oven 450°F

The garlic spread can be prepared up to an hour before ready to use.

Garlic Cheese Bread

1	loaf French bread
1	large garlic clove
½	cup butter, sliced
2	tablespoons shredded Cheddar cheese
2	tablespoons grated Parmesan cheese

Slice bread lengthwise and place on a baking sheet. Place garlic in a small food processor or blender and process to mince.

Add butter, Cheddar and Parmesan and process just until blended and smooth. Spread evenly on the bread and bake 4 to 5 minutes or until heated through and just beginning to crisp. Cut into diagonal slices and serve. Makes 10 to 12 servings.

Banana Bread

Oven 350°F

1	cup butter, softened
2	cups sugar
2	cups mashed very ripe bananas
4	large eggs, well beaten
2	teaspoons baking soda
2¼	cups flour

An old favorite. Serve hot with plenty of honey and butter. This continues to be one of my customers' favorite recipes.

In a large mixer bowl, cream butter and sugar. Add bananas and eggs. Combine baking soda and flour. Add to banana mixture; stirring by hand, until flour is moistened.

Pour batter into two sprayed 9x5x3-inch loaf pans. Bake 50 to 55 minutes or until tester inserted in center comes out clean. Run knife around edge and turn out immediately. Cool on rack. Makes 2 loaves.

The Basic Muffin

Oven 400°F

2	cups flour
½	cup sugar
1	tablespoon baking powder
5	tablespoons oil
1	egg
¾	cup milk

A basic muffin made different by your choice of variations.

Variations:
Add one or two of the following ingredients.

1   cup blueberries

½   cup dried cranberries

½   cup dried nuts

1   tablespoon freshly grated lemon or orange peel

Combine first 3 ingredients in a mixing bowl.

Combine remaining ingredients and add to dry mixture, stirring just until lightly moistened. Spoon into a sprayed muffin tin, filling ⅔ full. Bake 18 to 20 minutes or until lightly browned and center tests done. Makes 12 muffins.

If you like cornbread, you'll like this lighter, rather sweet version of one of our favorite recipes. If desired, you can add ½ cup fresh or frozen corn.

Really Quick Muffins

With most muffin recipes, you can save time by combining the dry ingredients in one bowl and the liquid ingredients in another bowl. Lightly spray muffin tins and set aside. When ready to bake, combine the ingredients and bake. You can also mix the dry ingredients in a resealable bag and store in pantry until ready to use.

Jiffy Cornbread Muffins

1	(8½-oz) box corn muffin mix
1	(8½-oz) box yellow cake mix
2	large eggs, lightly beaten
3	tablespoons vegetable oil
⅓	cup milk

Place both mixes in a medium mixing bowl. Stir to combine and to break up any lumps. Add eggs, oil, and milk, along with ½ cup water. Stir just until moistened. Spoon into a sprayed muffin tin. Bake 18 to 20 minutes or until tester inserted in center comes out clean. Makes 12 muffins.

Jalapeno Corn Muffins

1	(8½-oz) box corn muffin mix
1	large egg, lightly beaten
⅓	cup milk
¾	cup (3-oz) Monterey Jack cheese with peppers

Combine corn muffin mix, egg, and milk in a medium bowl, mixing just until moistened. Spoon into a sprayed muffin tin.

Cut cheese into 6 cubes. Place one in each muffin cup, pressing down with a spoon and making sure each is covered with batter. Bake 10 to 12 minutes or until golden and firm to the touch. Remove and serve hot. Makes 6 muffins.

Whole Wheat Muffins

Oven 375°F

2	cups whole wheat flour
½	cup sugar
3½	teaspoons baking powder
1	large egg, lightly beaten
3	tablespoons butter, melted
1½	cups milk

In large mixing bowl, combine first 3 ingredients. Combine remaining ingredients and add to dry mixture, stirring just until flour is moistened. Spoon into a sprayed muffin tin, filling ¾ full. Bake 25 to 30 minutes or until tester inserted in center comes out clean. Makes 12 muffins.

Tip: To prevent muffin tins from warping, fill any empty cups with water.

Tip: For a longer storage life, keep whole wheat flour in the freezer. Then remove amount needed and let come to room temperature before using.

Sally Lunn Muffins

Oven 400°F

½	cup butter, softened
⅓	cup sugar
1	large egg
3	teaspoons baking powder
1½	cups flour
¾	cup milk

In a mixer bowl, cream butter and sugar until thoroughly blended. Add egg and mix well. Combine baking powder and flour. Add to the creamed mixture alternately with the milk, starting and ending with flour.

Spoon into a sprayed muffin tin, filling ¾ full. Bake 18 to 20 minutes or until tester inserted in center comes out clean. Remove and place on rack. Best served right away. Makes 12 large muffins.

A wonderfully light, not too sweet muffin.

Blueberry Drop Biscuits

Serve these easy
to make biscuits
anytime. If desired,
substitute dried
cranberries for the
blueberries.

1	cup flour
½	teaspoon salt
1½	teaspoons baking powder
1	tablespoon butter, chilled
½	cup milk
½	cup fresh blueberries

Combine flour, salt, and baking powder in a mixing bowl. Cut in butter with two knives or a pastry blender. Add milk, stirring just enough to moisten. Carefully fold in blueberries. Drop by tablespoon onto a sprayed baking sheet. Bake 12 to 14 minutes or until lightly browned. Makes 12 biscuits.

Easy Pecan Rolls

Occasionally, we just
must have some-
thing to satisfy our
sweet tooth. I like to
make these on a lazy
Saturday morning
when I can linger
over a cup of hot cof-
fee and enjoy a roll
or two.

½	cup firmly packed brown sugar
½	cup butter, melted
36	to 48 pecan halves, depending on size
	Cinnamon
2	cups baking mix

Place 2 teaspoons brown sugar and 2 teaspoons melted butter in each of 12 muffin cups; stir to blend. Place 3 to 4 pecan halves in each cup. Sprinkle lightly with cinnamon.

Combine baking mix and ½ cup water until a soft dough forms; beat about 20 strokes. Spoon into muffin cups. Bake 8 to 10 minutes; watch carefully so they don't burn. Invert pan on waxed paper, leaving pan over rolls for about a minute. Makes 12 rolls.

Cakes, Desserts & Pies

Cranberry–Nut Cake

1   cup, plus 1 tablespoon sugar
1   cup flour
⅔   cup coarsely chopped pecans
2   cups cranberries
2   large eggs, lightly beaten
½   cup butter, melted

A quick cake that can be prepared in less than 10 minutes.

In a mixing bowl, combine the 1 cup sugar and flour. Add pecans and cranberries, tossing to coat. Add eggs and butter and stir until thoroughly mixed.

Pour into a sprayed 8x8-inch baking dish. Sprinkle the 1 tablespoon sugar evenly over the top. Bake 30 to 35 minutes or until tester inserted in center comes out clean. Serve warm or room temperature. Makes 6 to 8 servings.

Cake Tips

To make a good cake, you must follow a few simple rules. Unless you have made the cake before, you should follow the recipe exactly. Ingredients should be at room temperature. Use large size eggs and butter that contains at least 8 grams of saturated fat per tablespoon. Spray and flour the bottom only of cake pan. Fill the cake pan with batter, then hold pan a few inches above the counter and drop a few times to remove large air bubbles. Cool cake on a rack for 10 minutes, then remove the pan and allow to cool.

When you want to impress someone, but you don't have a lot of time to cook, make this quick and easy dessert using an Angel food cake mix. You'll be impressed with this beautiful cake and so will they. It also has an added bonus of being low in fat. Serve with ice cream or sweetened fresh strawberries.

Almond Angel Food Cake

1	(16-oz) box Angel food cake mix
1½	teaspoons almond extract, divided
1½	to 2 cups sifted powdered sugar
⅓	cup sliced almonds

Prepare cake according to directions on box, adding 1 teaspoon almond extract along with the water. Pour into an ungreased 10-inch angel food cake pan with removable bottom. Bake 38 to 45 minutes or until golden and tester inserted in center comes out clean. Invert pan and cool.

Combine 1½ cups powdered sugar with *2 tablespoons water* and the remaining ½ teaspoon almond extract. You want to be able to drizzle the frosting, so if too thin, add more powdered sugar. If too dry, add just a tiny bit more water. Drizzle over cake, allowing some of the frosting to drip over sides. Sprinkle top with almonds. Makes 12 servings.

You can fool anyone with this made from scratch taste - from a box.

Chocolate Cake 'n Peaches

1	(18.25-oz) box Devil's food cake mix
⅔	cup sour cream
2	large eggs
1	teaspoon almond extract
	Sliced peaches with syrup

In large mixer bowl, combine first four ingredients with *½ cup water*. Beat at low speed until combined. Continue to beat 2 minutes at medium speed.

Pour into a sprayed 10-inch springform pan and bake 40 to 45 minutes or until tester inserted in center comes out clean. Cool in pan 10 minutes. Remove ring and let cool on rack. Serve with peaches. Makes 12 servings.

Triple Fudge Cake

1	(3-oz) box regular chocolate pudding mix
2	cups milk
1	(18.25-oz) box Devils food cake mix
½	cup semi-sweet chocolate chips
½	cup chopped walnuts

This is a heavy spongy type cake, and is great for eating out of hand and for sack lunches.

Prepare pudding mix with milk as directed on box. Remove from heat; stir dry cake mix into hot pudding. Mixture will be quite thick and spongy.

Pour into a sprayed 13x9-inch pan. Sprinkle with chocolate chips and nuts and bake 30 to 35 minutes or until tester inserted in center comes out clean. Makes 12 servings.

Butter

All is not created equal

In testing recipes and in day-to-day cooking, we have experienced quite different results between brands of butter. We noticed that most of the quality butters contain 8 grams of saturated fat per tablespoon and the cheaper brands contain only 7 grams. This difference can have quite a dramatic result in some recipes.

The recipes most affected are candies, cakes, cookies and muffins. The higher fat content always produced the best results, and in some instances, the lower fat content butter caused the recipe to fail completely. To make things even more confusing, we did find one 7 gram brand that worked as well as the 8 gram.

I like to use the less expensive butter for table or non-baking use and save the more expensive butter for baking.

Coconut Pecan Cake

Menu:
Serve with scrambled
eggs, ham slices and
sliced tomatoes or
cantaloupe.

4	large eggs
1	(16-oz) box light brown sugar
½	cup vegetable oil
2	cups baking mix
1	(7-oz) package flaked coconut
1	cup chopped pecans or walnuts

In a mixer bowl, lightly beat the eggs. Add brown sugar and mix well. Stir in the oil. Add the baking mix, a small amount at a time and mix well. Stir in the coconut and nuts. Pour into an ungreased 13x9-inch baking pan and bake 35 to 45 minutes or until a tester inserted in center comes out clean. Let cool slightly, cut into squares. Makes 12 to 16 servings.

Raisin Walnut Cake

Don't be put off by the 1 cup mayonnaise. It actually takes the place of eggs and fat in the recipe and makes for a wonderfully moist cake that requires no frosting.

Variation:
Substitute 1 cup chopped dates for the raisins. For chocolate cake add 6 tablespoons (1½-oz) grated unsweetened chocolate.

1	cup raisins
1	cup chopped walnuts
2	teaspoons baking soda
1	cup sugar
1	cup mayonnaise
2	cups flour

Combine raisins, walnuts and baking soda in a large mixing bowl. Add *1 cup hot water* and set aside while measuring remaining ingredients.

Add sugar to raisin-nut mixture. Then stir in mayonnaise until blended. Stir in flour just until smooth. Pour into a lightly sprayed 13x9-inch baking dish. Bake 25 to 30 minutes or until a tester inserted in center comes out clean. Makes 12 servings.

Special Lunch Box Cake

Oven 350°F

2	cups sugar, divided
2	teaspoons baking soda
2	cups flour
2	large eggs, lightly beaten
1	(17-oz) can fruit cocktail, undrained
¾	cup coarsely chopped walnuts

In mixing bowl, combine 1½ cups of the sugar, baking soda and flour. Add eggs and fruit cocktail. Mix well and pour into a sprayed 13x9-inch baking pan. Sprinkle remaining ½ cup sugar evenly over top. Sprinkle with nuts. Bake 60 minutes or until a tester inserted in center comes out clean. Makes 12 servings.

Wrap individual slices in foil and freeze until ready to use.

Banana Cake

Oven 350°F

1	(18.25-oz) box yellow cake mix
¼	cup vegetable oil
4	large eggs
1½	cups mashed very ripe bananas, about 3 large
¾	cup chopped walnuts

In a mixer bowl, combine cake mix, oil, eggs and *1 cup water*. Beat until well mixed, about 2 to 3 minutes. Stir in the bananas and nuts. Pour into a sprayed 13x9-inch baking pan and bake 25 to 30 minutes or until a cake tester inserted in center comes out clean. Place on rack and cool. Makes 12 to 16 servings.

You really don't need a frosting with this cake, but for those die-hard frosting lovers, try the Cream Cheese Frosting on page 54.

I love those little boxes of cake mixes. They are so convenient to have on hand when you don't really want a large cake or dessert.

Coconut Snack Cake

1	(9-oz) box yellow cake mix
1	large egg
1½	cups flaked coconut
½	cup packed light brown sugar
1	teaspoon vanilla extract
5	tablespoons heavy cream or evaporated milk

Combine cake mix with the egg and ½ *cup water* as directed on box. Pour into a sprayed 8x8-inch baking dish and bake 18 to 20 minutes or until tester inserted in center comes out clean. Place on a rack and allow to cool 10 minutes.

Combine remaining ingredients and carefully spread over cake. Place under broiler and broil about 2 minutes or until lightly browned (watch carefully, it can burn very quickly). Let cool. Makes 9 servings.

Brownie fans will enjoy these. For variety, add 1¼ cups coarsely chopped walnuts to the batter or sprinkle the top of each cupcake with walnuts before baking.

Brownie Cupcakes

1	cup butter, softened
⅔	cup semi-sweet chocolate chips
1¾	cups sugar
4	large eggs
1	teaspoon vanilla extract
1	cup flour

Melt butter and chocolate chips in a medium saucepan over low heat. Stir in sugar; mix well. Add eggs, vanilla and flour. Stir until blended and smooth. Pour into cupcake liners, filling ¾ full. Bake 25 to 30 minutes or until tester inserted in center is just slightly moist. Makes 16 cupcakes.

Mom's Fruitcake

1	cup mixed candied fruit
2	teaspoons baking soda
1	cup sugar
1	cup mayonnaise
1	cup chopped pecans
2	cups flour

Place the candied fruit in a 2 cup measuring cup. Sprinkle baking soda over top. Add just enough warm water to cover the fruit. Set aside.

In medium bowl, combine sugar, mayonnaise and nuts. Add candied fruit mixture. Stir in the flour. Pour into a lightly sprayed 13x9-inch baking pan. Bake 30 to 35 minutes or until tester inserted in center comes out clean. Makes 12 servings.

Note: It's no wonder that a lot of people don't care for candied fruit or citron. Too often the brands carried in the supermarkets are inferior and dry. Good candied fruit should be fresh and moist. Often you can find this at your delicatessens, especially Italian ones. The last time I made this cake for my family I couldn't find candied mixed fruit, so I used chopped glazed red and green cherries I happened to have in the freezer. It was very good, the cake was moist, and even my grandchildren ate Great Grandma Warren's "fruitcake."

Oven 350°F

This is the fruitcake my brothers and I grew up on; then I went on to make the fancier kinds. I hadn't made this one for years, but am now enjoying it all over again. It's very easy to make, you don't even have to get out your mixer and frosting isn't necessary.

Cake Mix Tip

For a more "from scratch flavor," add ½ teaspoon butter extract and ½ teaspoon vanilla extract to purchased cake mixes.

Blueberry Coffee Cake

This cake is best
served same day
made.

2	cups flour
1	teaspoon baking powder
4	large eggs, lightly beaten
1	cup vegetable oil
1	cup sugar
1	(21-oz) can blueberry pie filling

Combine flour and baking powder in a mixer bowl. Add next 3 ingredients and mix until smooth. Spread half the batter in a sprayed 13x9-inch baking pan; the layer will be thin. Spoon pie filling evenly over top. Pour remaining batter over top and gently spread to cover the filling. Bake 35 to 45 minutes or until a tester inserted in center comes out clean. Serve warm. Makes 12 to 16 servings.

Eggnog Cake

A very good light-
textured cake made
even better with a
scoop of vanilla ice
cream. Purchase a
cake mix without the
pudding added. If
the cake is for com-
pany, lightly dust the
top with powdered
sugar or garnish with
fresh fruit.

1	(18.25-oz) box yellow cake mix
¼	teaspoon nutmeg
¼	cup butter, melted
1½	cups purchased eggnog
2	large eggs
½	teaspoon rum extract

Brush a 10-inch tube cake pan or Bundt pan with shortening. Sprinkle with flour; shake off excess.

Combine all the ingredients in a mixer bowl and beat until blended. Then beat on medium speed until batter is smooth, about 2 minutes.

Pour batter into prepared pan and bake 45 to 55 minutes or until tester inserted in center comes out clean. Cool in pan 10 minutes. Remove from pan; cool on rack. Makes 10 to 12 servings.

Blueberry Orange Cake

Oven 350°F

2	oranges
1	(18.25-oz) box lemon cake mix
⅓	cup vegetable oil
3	large eggs
1½	cups fresh or frozen blueberries

So moist you don't need frosting or ice cream. Perfect with a cup of coffee.

Wash oranges and grate 1 tablespoon peel. Squeeze oranges to make ½ cup juice. Place orange peel and juice in a large mixer bowl.

Add cake mix, oil, eggs and ½ cup water. Beat on low about 1 minute to combine ingredients. Beat on medium speed for 2 minutes. By hand, carefully fold in the blueberries. Pour into a sprayed 13x9-inch baking dish. Bake 30 to 40 minutes or until a tester inserted in center comes out clean. Place on rack to cool. Makes 12 servings.

Pineapple Cake

Oven 350°F

2	larges eggs, lightly beaten
1	(20-oz) can crushed pineapple, undrained
2	teaspoons baking soda
2	cups sugar
2	cups flour
1	cup chopped walnuts or pecans

Oil is not used in this recipe, making it somewhat lower in fat.

In a large bowl, combine eggs and pineapple. Combine baking soda, sugar and flour and add to egg mixture. Mix until well blended.

Pour into a sprayed 13x9-inch baking dish. Bake 40 to 45 minutes or until a tester inserted in center comes out clean. Let cool. Makes 12 servings.

Note: Cake can be frosted or served with ice cream or whipped cream.

Forget layer cakes. This cake is easy to frost and pretty when sliced and served. Frost with your favorite white frosting and sprinkle with coconut.

Dome Cake

1	(18.25-oz) box German chocolate cake mix
3	large eggs
1	cup sour cream
¼	cup oil
1	(1-oz) bottle red food coloring
	Frosting of choice

In a large mixer bowl, combine all ingredients along with *½ cup water*. Beat at low speed until moistened. Then beat at medium speed for 2 minutes. Pour into a sprayed round 10-cup ovenproof glass or metal bowl and bake 55 to 60 minutes or until a tester inserted in the center comes out clean. Place on rack and cool 15 minutes. Remove and cool on rack. Makes 12 servings.

My brothers and I loved it when Mom made this cake. We always knew we were in for a special treat.

Tip: For easier mixing, make sure the orange juice concentrate has thoroughly thawed, and is at room temperature.

Mom's Orange Cake

1	(18.25-oz) box white cake mix with pudding
1	(3-oz) box lemon gelatin
4	large eggs
¾	cup vegetable oil
3½	cups sifted powdered sugar
1	(6-oz) can frozen orange juice concentrate, thawed

In a mixer bowl, combine the cake mix, gelatin, eggs, oil and *¾ cup water*. Beat about 2 minutes or until smooth and thoroughly mixed. Pour into a sprayed deep 13x9-inch baking pan. Bake for 30 to 40 minutes or until a tester inserted in the center comes out clean. Let cool on rack 10 minutes.

Meanwhile, combine powdered sugar and orange juice and beat until smooth. When cake has cooled slightly, poke holes all the way to the bottom, using a kitchen fork or a skewer. Pour glaze over cake and spread to cover. Let cool. Makes 12 to 16 servings.

Common Yields & Measurements

4 ounces cheese	1 cup, shredded
16 ounces cheese	4 cups, shredded
3 ounces cream cheese	6 tablespoons
8 ounces cream cheese	1 cup
1 pound butter	2 cups (4 sticks)
1 cup heavy cream	2 cups whipped
1 pound all-purpose flour	4 cups, sifted
1 pound granulated sugar	2 cups
1 pound powdered sugar	3½ cups
1 pound brown sugar	2¼-2½ cups, packed
1 ounce unsweetened chocolate	1 square
12 ounce package chocolate chips	2 cups

The mayonnaise takes the place of oil in this recipe.

Chocolate Fudge Cake

1   (18.25-oz) box Chocolate Fudge cake mix
½   cup cocoa
3   large eggs
1   cup mayonnaise
1   cup semi-sweet chocolate chips
     Vanilla ice cream

In mixer bowl, combine cake mix and cocoa. Beat in the eggs and mayonnaise while gradually adding *1⅓ cups water*. Beat about 2 minutes to blend. Stir in chocolate chips. Pour into a sprayed Bundt cake pan and bake 40 to 50 minutes or until a tester inserted in center comes out clean. Cool 10 minutes, then remove and cool. Makes 12 servings.

You'll enjoy this beautiful cake when fresh plums are in season. This not-too-sweet dessert is wonderful with a steaming cup of coffee. Best eaten the same day made.

Plum Cake

½   cup butter, softened
⅓   cup sugar
1   (8-oz) can almond paste
2   large eggs, lightly beaten
1   cup flour
3   medium-firm red or black plums

In a mixer bowl, combine butter, sugar and almond paste. Beat until mixture is thoroughly blended and smooth. Add eggs and beat until well mixed and has a fluffy consistency. Add flour and beat on medium until blended.

Pour into a sprayed 10-inch springform pan. Cut plums in half, then each half into four wedges. Arrange in an attractive pattern over cake batter. Bake 40 to 45 minutes or until lightly browned. Let cool 10 to 15 minutes before removing rim. Serve warm or room temperature. Makes 8 servings.

Mini Pineapple Cakes

1   (8-oz) can crushed pineapple, drained, save juice
½   cup butter, partially melted
½   cup packed light brown sugar
5   maraschino cherries, halved
1   (12-oz) package refrigerated biscuits.

Combine pineapple, butter, and brown sugar. Spoon into 10 sprayed muffin cups. Place a cherry half, rounded side down on top.

Place a biscuit on top. Brush with some of the pineapple juice. Bake 12 to 15 minutes or until golden (the outside of the biscuits should be a little crunchy.) Makes 10 servings.

These are delicious little gems! And so easy to make.

Pineapple Upside-Down Cake

Oven 350°F

1   (18-oz) box white cake mix
⅓   cup vegetable oil
3   large eggs
6   canned pineapple rings, drained (two 8-oz cans)
6   maraschino cherries, drained
1   cup chopped pecans or walnuts, divided

In mixer bowl, combine the cake mix, oil, eggs and the amount of water called for in the mix. Beat 30 seconds to mix; then beat on medium-high for 2 minutes.

Meanwhile, arrange pineapples in bottom of a sprayed 10-inch springform pan. (Spray bottom only.) Place a cherry in center of each. Sprinkle with ½ cup of the nuts. Pour batter over top. Sprinkle remaining ½ cup nuts over batter. Bake 40 to 45 minutes or until a tester inserted in center comes out clean. Let cool 10 minutes before turning out on rack to cool. Makes 10 to 12 servings.

Want a dessert, but don't have a lot of time? This cake can be mixed and ready for the oven in less than 10 minutes.

Note: The yellow cake mixes have changed over the last few years. So I prefer using white mix with whole eggs rather than egg whites.

Cherry Almond Cake

The mixing method in this recipe is different than most, but still easy to make.

Variation:
Cake can be sprinkled with powdered sugar or served with whipped cream or ice cream - this makes it very rich.

¼	cup vegetable oil
1	(18.25-oz) box yellow cake mix
2	large eggs
¾	teaspoon almond extract
1	(20-oz) can cherry pie filling

Pour oil in a 13x9-inch baking dish, tilting to cover the bottom.

In a mixing bowl, combine cake mix, eggs and almond extract with *½ cup water*, blending with a fork. Spread evenly in baking dish.

Spoon pie filling onto batter. Stir lightly with a fork to create a marble effect. Bake 30 to 40 minutes or until center tests done, serve warm. Makes 12 servings.

Room Temperature Butter

If you are in a hurry and you need the butter at room temperature - microwaving it just doesn't do a very good job. The butter is melted on the inside and still cold on the outside. To get butter to room temperature quickly, simply place a cube between wax paper and roll to about a ¼-inch thickness. By the time you measure out the remaining ingredients the butter should be ready.

Chocolate Cake

2	cups flour
1	cup sugar
¼	cup cocoa
2	teaspoons baking soda
1	cup mayonnaise
1	teaspoon vanilla extract

In mixer bowl, combine the flour, sugar, cocoa, and baking soda. Add mayonnaise, vanilla and *1½ cups water*. Beat on medium speed about one minute or until well mixed and smooth. Pour into a sprayed 13x9-inch baking pan. Bake 25 to 30 minutes or until a tester inserted in center comes out clean. Makes 12 servings.

Family Favorite Chocolate Frosting

¼	cup milk
¼	cup butter
1	cup semi-sweet chocolate chips
1	teaspoon vanilla extract
2½	cups sifted powdered sugar

Combine milk and butter in a small saucepan. Bring to a boil; remove from heat. Add chocolate chips and stir until smooth.

Place chocolate mixture, vanilla extract and powdered sugar in a mixer bowl. Beat until spreading consistency. If necessary, thin with a few drops of milk.

Oven 350°F

This popular moist chocolate cake is perfect for a picnic or potluck dinner. The mayonnaise takes the place of the eggs and the oil in the recipe.

Note: Frost with one of your favorite frostings.

Stove Top

My absolute favorite chocolate frosting. Don't add too much powdered sugar, because the frosting will thicken as it cools. Makes enough frosting for a 13x9-inch or 2 layer cake.

Buttercream Frosting

The frosting can be changed by substituting different liquids for the milk such as lemon or orange juice, coffee, chocolate, etc.

¼	cup butter, softened
3	cups sifted powdered sugar
1	teaspoon vanilla extract
3	to 4 tablespoons milk

In a small mixer bowl, cream the butter until smooth. Add sugar, vanilla and 3 tablespoons milk. Beat until creamy and thick enough to spread. It may be necessary to add more milk or powdered sugar to get the desired consistency. Makes enough frosting for a 13x9-inch cake.

Powdered Sugar Glaze

If too thin, add additional sugar; if too thick, thin with water.

1	cup sifted powdered sugar
1	tablespoon hot water
1½	teaspoons light corn syrup
¼	teaspoon vanilla extract

Combine ingredients in small mixing bowl; stir until smooth.

Cream Cheese Frosting

This is a delicious frosting for carrot or lemon cake. Because of the cream cheese, it must be kept refrigerated.

1	(8-oz) package cream cheese, softened
½	cup butter, softened
1	teaspoon vanilla extract
1	(16-oz) box of powdered sugar

In mixer bowl, beat cream cheese until smooth. Add butter and vanilla and beat until mixed. Add powdered sugar, beating until smooth.

Quick Ice Cream Desserts

Grilled fresh pineapple slices with vanilla ice cream

Lemon sherbet or sorbet with sweetened raspberries

Vanilla ice cream and orange sherbet with a tablespoon of Amaretto and a crisp butter cookie

Vanilla or chocolate swirl ice cream with sweetened sliced peaches

Layer vanilla ice cream and crushed Oreos®

Layer crushed vanilla wafers, vanilla ice cream and crushed toffee bars

Brownies topped with ice cream and chocolate sauce

Angel Food Cake with ice cream and sliced mixed fruit

Layer ice cream with caramel sauce, then top with crushed toffee bars, nuts, or toasted coconut

Vanilla Sherbet Dessert

1	pint vanilla ice cream, softened slightly
1	pint pineapple sherbet
2	teaspoons fresh orange zest
1½	tablespoons Grand Marnier liqueur
⅓	cup toasted flaked coconut

In a large mixer bowl, combine the first four ingredients; beat just until smooth and blended. Spoon into parfait or wine glasses. Sprinkle with toasted coconut. Makes 6 servings.

Tip: Leftover mixture can be frozen. It will be firmer, but is equally as delicious. Make the dessert just before serving, but toast the coconut ahead of time.

Rice Chex® Dessert

2½	cups crushed Rice Chex cereal
1	cup firmly packed light brown sugar
1	cup cashews, split
½	cup butter, melted
1	cup flaked coconut
½	gallon vanilla ice cream, softened

Combine first 5 ingredients; mix thoroughly. Spread half of mixture evenly in buttered 13x9-inch baking dish; pat down. Spread ice cream evenly over top. Sprinkle remaining cereal mixture over ice cream; pat lightly.

Cover and freeze. When ready to serve, remove from freezer and cut into squares. Makes 12 to 15 servings.

Freeze

This recipe is worth the price of the cookbook. If strawberries are in season, it looks pretty to top each serving with a strawberry and a mint leaf.

Ice Cream & Strawberries

Vanilla ice cream
Sliced almonds
Sliced sweetened strawberries

Make desired number of ice cream balls. Quickly roll in almonds and place each in a muffin tin. Cover with plastic wrap and freeze until ready to use. Place each in a dessert dish and top with strawberries.

Variations:
- Ice cream, coconut, hot fudge sauce
- Ice cream, sliced almonds, hot fudge sauce
- Ice cream, chopped pecans, chocolate sauce
- Ice cream, coconut, sweetened raspberries

Freeze

Keep some of the ice cream balls in the freezer for quick entertaining, but wrap tightly to prevent the ice cream from drying out.

Strawberry Shortcake

1	(10.2-oz) can Grands® biscuits
¼	cup butter, melted
¼	cup sugar
1	tablespoon sliced almonds (optional)
	Fresh strawberries, sliced, sweetened

Dip each biscuit in melted butter and then into sugar to coat. Place on ungreased baking sheet. Sprinkle a few almonds over each biscuit. Bake 15 to 18 minutes or until cooked through and golden. Serve warm topped with strawberries. Makes 5 servings.

Oven 375°F

This is a wonderfully delicious way to use up those biscuits before the expiration date.

Coconut Custard

4	large eggs, lightly beaten
⅓	cup sugar
½	teaspoon vanilla extract
1	cup heavy cream
¼	cup flaked coconut
	Nutmeg

Combine eggs, sugar, and vanilla. Mix cream with *2 cups water* and gradually add to egg mixture. Stir in coconut.

Place 6 ungreased 10-oz ramekins in a 13x9-inch baking dish. Fill ramekins. Sprinkle lightly with nutmeg.

Fill baking dish with 1-inch of boiling water. Carefully place dish in oven. Bake 30 to 40 minutes or until center is just set (still some jiggle left). Let cool on rack. Cover with plastic wrap and chill in refrigerator. Makes 6 servings.

Oven 325°F
Chill

A nice creamy custard and a great make ahead dessert.

Easy Brownie Towers

There are times when
you may want a
special dessert, but
you just don't have
a lot of time to cook.
Since mixes vary, use
ingredients called for
on the box.

Brownie mix or prepared brownies
Vanilla ice cream
Caramel or chocolate sauce, slightly heated
Chopped nuts, if desired

Prepare brownie mix as instructed on box. Let cool and
cut into serving size squares. Place on a serving plate and
top each with a scoop of ice cream. Drizzle the dessert and
some of the plate with the sauce. And for drama (we all need
a little drama in our lives, don't we?) sprinkle with a little
powdered sugar.

Family Favorite Toffee Delight

Freeze

When in their teens,
this is the dessert my
children wanted for
their birthday cake.
In fact, they still do.
Just add candles.

Note: If you wish
to make a smaller
dessert, use half the
ingredients and a
9x5-inch loaf pan
lined with foil (for
easy removal).
My favorite dessert?
If I had to choose
one, this would be it.

1½	packages soft-type Ladyfingers, split
1	to 1½ quarts chocolate ice cream, softened
1	to 1½ quarts vanilla ice cream, softened
10	Heath® bars, coarsely crushed

Line sides and bottom of Angel food cake pan (with removable bottom) with Ladyfingers, rounded side out. Half fill
pan with chocolate ice cream. Sprinkle half of the crushed
candy over top. Add vanilla ice cream; sprinkle with remaining candy.

Cover with foil and freeze. Makes 12 to 14 servings.

Brownie Delight

1	box fudge brownie mix
1	quart vanilla ice cream, softened
½	cup chopped pecans
2	to 3 cups sliced strawberries
¼	cup sugar or to taste

Prepare brownie mix as directed on box using a sprayed 13x9-inch baking dish. Cool completely.

Spread ice cream over brownies. Sprinkle with pecans. Cover and freeze.

Meanwhile, combine strawberries and sugar. Cover and chill 1 to 2 hours. When ready to serve, cut into squares and top with strawberries and some of the juice. Makes 12 servings.

Peach & Raspberry Dessert

2	cups fresh raspberries
¼	cup sugar or to taste
4	white peaches, peeled and sliced
1	pint vanilla ice cream

Sweeten raspberries with sugar to taste. Place in blender and blend just until smooth. Press mixture through a sieve to remove the seeds. Place peach slices in four dessert dishes. Top with a scoop of ice cream, then top with raspberry sauce. Makes 4 servings.

Oven 350°F
Freeze-Chill

This combination of everyone's favorite ingredients, brownies and strawberries, is a "delight." You can use any brownie mix you have on hand, but in keeping with Six Ingredients or Less, use a mix that requires water only. Omit strawberries, if not in season, and you still have a wonderful dessert.

White peaches (during season) are showing up in more and more grocery stores today.

You can always impress your guests with this easy, but deliciously attractive dessert.

Hawaiian Delight Cheesecake

2	(3-oz) packages soft Ladyfingers
2	(8-oz) packages cream cheese, softened
½	cup sugar
1	(20-oz) can crushed pineapple, well drained
1	(8-oz) container frozen whipped topping, thawed
½	cup flaked coconut, toasted

You will love the convenience of no-bake cheesecakes.

Note: To prevent tiny lumps, make sure the cream cheese is quite soft; then beat thoroughly before adding the pineapple.

Tip: If you can't find a small 8-oz container of whipped topping, or if you already have a larger container on hand, measure 3½ cups for this recipe.

Place ladyfingers, rounded-side out, around the sides and bottom of a 9-inch springform pan. Fill in with smaller pieces where needed; you will have a few of the ladyfingers left over.

Beat cream cheese until soft. Gradually add the sugar and beat until fluffy. Stir in pineapple and fold in whipped topping. Pour into pan and spread the top until smooth. Sprinkle with coconut. Cover with plastic wrap. Chill overnight or at least several hours. Makes 8 to 10 servings.

Party Time!

I gave a little tea party

This afternoon at three

"Twas very small - three guests in all

I, myself and me

Myself ate up the sandwiches

While I drank all the tea

'Twas also I who ate the pie

and passed the cake to me

Author unknown

Lemon Cheesecake

Chill

1	(3-oz) box lemon gelatin
2	(8-oz) packages cream cheese, softened
½	cup sugar
½	cup sour cream
¼	cup heavy cream
1	graham cracker pie crust

Thoroughly mix the lemon gelatin with ¼ *cup boiling water*, stirring until dissolved.

In mixer bowl, combine remaining ingredients and beat until smooth and light. Add gelatin and beat until smooth. Pour into pie crust. Chill 3 to 4 hours or until set. Makes 12 servings

This is good. Creamy with a light touch of lemon. Garnish with whipped cream and thin strands of lemon peel.

Quick Cheesecake Toppings

Blueberry sauce
Assorted fresh fruit
Chocolate sauce sprinkled with sliced almonds
Orange marmalade with Grand Marnier to taste
Melted seedless raspberry or blackberry jam
Caramel sauce
Shaved white chocolate

A purchased cheesecake served with your choice of toppings is a lifesaver for the busy host or hostess.

Keep these ingredients on hand for a delicious make ahead dessert.

Pistachio Dessert

50	Ritz® crackers, crushed
½	cup butter, melted
1	quart vanilla ice cream, softened
1	cup milk
1	(3.4-oz) package instant pistachio pudding mix
1	(8-oz) container frozen whipped topping, thawed

Combine cracker crumbs and butter. Pat evenly into a sprayed 13x9-inch baking dish. Bake 10 to 15 minutes. Remove from oven and let cool.

In mixer bowl, blend ice cream, milk, and pudding mix. Pour over crust. Spread whipped topping over top. Chill several hours or overnight. Makes 10 to 12 servings.

Easy Party Cake

1	Angel food cake
2	cups whipping cream
¼	cup sugar
3	cups sliced strawberries, with sugar to taste

Whip cream, adding ¼ cup sugar or more to taste. Frost cake with the whipped cream.

To serve, slice cake and spoon strawberries over top. Makes 10 servings.

If time permits, try using a cake mix instead of a store-bought cake. It is so much better and takes only minutes to mix.

Fruit Kabobs with Chocolate Sauce

Stove Top

4	small strawberries
4	cantaloupe cubes
4	pineapple chunks
4	large raspberries
	Chocolate sauce

Alternate fruit on small skewers, using 1 piece of each fruit.

Spoon 2 tablespoons sauce on dessert plates, tilting to coat somewhat. Place a fruit kabob in center of each plate. Drizzle each with 1 tablespoon chocolate. Makes 4 servings.

Serve as a light dessert after a heavy meal.

Apple Raspberry Crisp

Oven 350°F

8	cups peeled, sliced apples (4 to 5 large)
1	cup fresh or frozen raspberries
½	teaspoon cinnamon
¾	cup flour
1	cup sugar
⅓	cup cold butter

Place apple slices in a sprayed 11x7-inch baking dish. Distribute raspberries over top. Sprinkle *3 tablespoons water* over fruit. Sprinkle with cinnamon.

In a small mixing bowl, combine the cinnamon, flour, and sugar. Cut in butter with a pastry blender or two knives. Sprinkle over fruit. Bake 50 to 55 minutes or until light golden and apples are cooked through. Makes 8 servings.

The raspberries add a nice touch of color and taste. If you want a really scrumptious dessert, top with a scoop of vanilla ice cream or frozen yogurt.

Variation:
Use blueberries, pears, or dried cranberries in place of the raspberries. Or omit the raspberries and use just the apples.

Deep Dish Fruit Cobbler

½ cup butter, melted
1 cup baking mix
1 cup sugar
1 cup milk
1 quart fruit, drained (peaches, blackberries, etc.)

This recipe has been in our family for more years than I remember, but at least two generations. It is still one of our favorite desserts. Serve it warm with vanilla ice cream.

Pour butter into an 11x7-inch baking dish. Stir in baking mix, sugar, and milk. Pour fruit over top. Bake 35 to 40 minutes or until golden brown. Makes 6 servings.

Cantaloupe Sundaes

1 small cantaloupe
Vanilla ice cream

A great refreshingly light dessert. If dieting, use your favorite sugar free or low-carb ice cream. Garnish with blueberries if desired.

Cut cantaloupe in half and scoop out the seeds. Fill center with a scoop of ice cream. Makes 2 servings.

Note: If cantaloupe is large, or for smaller servings, cut into fourths.

Festive Serving Dish

My favorite pottery dish cost less than six dollars and can be found in the garden department of most home center stores. It is 10-inches across and about 2 to 2½-inches deep. It is the terra cotta saucer used for large planting pots. Purchase the ones that are glazed and be sure to do a lead test. I use them not only for pies, but also for yeast rolls, casseroles and potato dishes.

Apple Peach Cobbler

Oven 350°F

1	(21-oz) can apple pie filling
1	(29-oz) can sliced peaches, drained
1	(9-oz) box yellow cake mix
¼	cup butter, cut into small thin pieces

Spoon pie filling into a sprayed 8x8-inch baking dish. Add peaches and stir to mix.

Sprinkle cake mix evenly over the top and dot with the butter. Bake 40 to 50 minutes or until the topping is golden. Makes 6 servings.

Tip: Don't substitute more peaches for the pie filling since the pie filling acts as the thickener for the cobbler.

I hope you enjoy this cobbler type dessert. It takes less than 5 minutes to assemble and have ready for the oven.

Croissant Bread Pudding

Oven 350°F

2½	cups Half and Half
6	large eggs, lightly beaten
¾	cup sugar, divided
½	teaspoon cinnamon
8	croissants (day old works best)
¾	cup raisins

Combine Half and Half with the eggs. Combine ½ cup of the sugar with the cinnamon; add to egg mixture. Pour into a sprayed 11x7-inch baking dish.

Tear croissants into bite-size pieces. You should have about 7 cups. Add to custard, pressing down to cover. Sprinkle raisins over top. Sprinkle remaining ¼ cup sugar over raisins. Bake 40 to 50 minutes or until set. Serve warm with a little additional cream. Makes 6 servings.

A friend made this recipe for her husband and he ate the whole thing. (Not in one sitting, of course.)

Quick Company Desserts

Top fresh pineapple rings with a scoop of vanilla ice cream and sweetened strawberries or raspberries.

Make an ice cream sundae by using scoops of vanilla ice cream topped with fresh pineapple cubes, sliced bananas and a drizzle of Grand Marnier or Amaretto. Top with whipped cream and garnish with toasted coconut.

Top Pound cake or Angel food cake slices with sweetened mixed fruit, and if desired, garnish with a dollop of whipped cream.

Make brownies in a deep dish pizza pan. Cut into pie shape wedges and serve with ice cream and chocolate sauce.

Top purchased cheesecake slices with your favorite blueberry sauce recipe.

Roll vanilla ice cream into serving size balls, then roll in crushed toffee candy bars. Place in muffin tins and freeze. When ready to serve, place in dessert dishes and drizzle with hot fudge sauce.

Kettle Corn

Stove Top

¼   **cup oil**
¼   **cup sugar**
½   **cup popcorn kernels**

Combine oil and sugar and pour into a large pot.

Add popcorn. Cover. Cook over medium heat. As soon as it starts to pop, shake the pot constantly. Once popping has slowed, immediately remove popcorn to a serving bowl.

Craving kettle corn? Make your own with this quick delicious recipe. (Don't use microwave popcorn.)

Chocolate Grape Clusters

Stove Top
Chill

You will need:
  Milk chocolate
  Green grapes, separated into small clusters of 3 to 5 grapes

In a small saucepan, melt enough chocolate so that you can easily dip the grape clusters. Dip each cluster individually, turning to coat.

Place clusters on a wax paper lined shallow pan and chill until set. Store in refrigerator until ready to serve. Best served same day made.

If you like chocolate covered strawberries (and who doesn't) you will love these little gems.

Peanut Butter Pie

1	(9-inch) baked pie crust
1	(8-oz) package cream cheese, softened
1	cup creamy peanut butter
1	cup sugar
2	tablespoons butter, melted
1	cup whipping cream

In mixer bowl, beat the cream cheese until smooth. Add peanut butter, sugar and butter; beat until smooth. Whip the cream and add to peanut butter mixture; mix well. Pour into pie crust. Chill until firm. Makes 6 to 8 servings.

Amazing Coconut Pie

3	large eggs
¼	cup butter
1½	teaspoons vanilla extract
1	(14-oz) can sweetened condensed milk
½	cup baking mix
1	cup flaked coconut

In blender or mixer, combine first 5 ingredients along with *1½ cups water*; mix well. Pour into a sprayed deep-dish 10-inch pie plate. Sprinkle coconut over top. Bake 40 to 45 minutes or until mixture is set and knife inserted just off center comes out clean. Chill. Makes 6 to 8 servings.

Mile High Toffee Pie

1	(9-inch) baked pie crust
1	quart chocolate ice cream, softened
¾	quart vanilla ice cream, softened
½	cup crushed toffee candy bars

Spoon chocolate ice cream into pie crust. Sprinkle with toffee. Spoon vanilla ice cream over top. Freeze. Cover until ready to serve. Makes 8 to 10 servings

Peppermint Ice Cream Pie

1	(9-inch) baked pie crust
1	quart peppermint ice cream
⅓	cup chocolate sauce
2	cups frozen whipped topping, thawed
⅓	cup chopped pecans or walnuts

Spoon ice cream into pie crust leaving small dips for chocolate sauce.

Pour chocolate sauce over the ice cream. Spread with whipped topping. Sprinkle with nuts. Serve immediately or freeze until ready to serve. Makes 6 servings.

Freeze

If desired, top with chocolate sauce and whipped cream.

Variation:
Add toffee and ½ cup pecans to the vanilla ice cream.

Freeze

Variation:
Try different ice creams, toppings and nuts. Toasted coconut would also be good.

Pecan Crunch Pie

3	large egg whites
1	cup sugar
1	teaspoon baking powder
1	teaspoon vanilla extract
1	cup crushed graham cracker crumbs
1	cup chopped pecans

Beat egg whites until stiff. Combine sugar and baking powder; beat into egg whites. Add vanilla. Fold in graham cracker crumbs, then pecans. Pour into buttered 9-inch pie plate. Bake 30 minutes or until cooked through. Cool. Makes 6 servings.

Apple Crumb Pie

1	(9-inch) unbaked pie crust
6	to 7 tart apples, peeled and sliced
1	cup sugar, divided
1	teaspoon cinnamon
¾	cup flour
⅓	cup butter

Arrange apple slices in pie shell. Combine ½ cup sugar and cinnamon; sprinkle over apples.

Combine remaining sugar and flour in a small bowl. With two knives or a pastry blender, cut in butter until crumbly. Sprinkle over apples. Cover pie with foil and bake 30 minutes. Uncover and bake 10 minutes or until apples are tender. Makes 6 servings.

Fresh Strawberry Pie

1   (9-inch) baked pie shell
1   cup sugar
1   cup water, divided
3   tablespoons cornstarch
3   tablespoons strawberry gelatin
3   to 4 cups fresh whole small strawberries

Place sugar in a small saucepan. In a small bowl, combine ¼ cup of the water with the cornstarch, stirring until smooth. Add to saucepan along with the remaining ¾ cup water; mix well. Cook over medium-low heat until thickened, stirring frequently. Stir in the gelatin.

Line pie shell with strawberries, pointed end up. Fill in where necessary with smaller berries. Pour sauce over top. Chill until set. Makes 6 servings.

Stove Top Chill

Try to make the pie when local berries are available. They are more uniform in size and much more flavorful.

Busy Day Pumpkin Pie

1   (9-inch) unbaked pie crust
1   (16-oz) can pumpkin (not pie filling)
1   (14-oz) can sweetened condensed milk
1   large egg
1   teaspoon pumpkin pie spice
1   teaspoon cinnamon

Combine first 5 ingredients and blend well. Pour into pie crust. Bake 50 to 55 minutes or until knife inserted just off center comes out clean. Let cool, then place in refrigerator until ready to serve. Makes 6 servings.

Oven 375°F Chill

This is one of those recipes that is even better the second day.

Oven 350°F
Chill

If you like key lime pie, you will enjoy this recipe. I had an abundance of lemons, so I substituted lemons for the limes. When ready to serve, top with the sweetened whipped cream and garnish with fresh lemon peel or fresh berries, if desired.

Oven 350°F
Chill

Key Lime pie is quite rich with a citrus tart flavor that is just perfect after a special meal. You can use a pastry or graham cracker crust, or try the Pretzel Crust on page 77. Serve with whipped cream and/or assorted fresh fruit.

Quick Lemon Pie

1	(9-inch) baked pie crust
5	large egg yolks
1	(14-oz) can sweetened condensed milk
6	tablespoons fresh lemon juice
1	cup heavy cream, whipped with sugar to taste

Beat egg yolks lightly with a whisk. Gradually stir in the condensed milk, beating until smooth. Whisk in the lemon juice. Pour into pie shell. Cover pie with foil (this prevents crust from over browning) and bake for 10 minutes. Remove foil and bake 5 to 6 minutes. The filling should be set. Cool on rack. Chill until ready to serve. Serve each slice with a dollop of whipped cream. Makes 6 to 8 servings.

Key Lime Pie

1	(9-inch) baked pie crust
½	cup lime juice (4 to 5 limes)
2	teaspoons grated lime peel
4	large egg yolks
1	(14-oz) can sweetened condensed milk

Combine lime juice, zest, egg yolks and condensed milk, mixing until blended and smooth. Pour into pie crust. Bake 15 minutes or until center is just set. Let cool on rack, then chill until ready to serve. Makes 6 servings.

Dreamsicle Pie

1¾   **cups chocolate wafer cookie crumbs**
¼   **cup butter, melted**
1   **quart vanilla ice cream, softened**
1   **quart orange sherbet, softened**

Crush wafers in blender or food processor. Reserve 1 teaspoon for top. Add melted butter; mix to blend. Press into bottom and sides of a deep 9-inch pie pan. Spread half of vanilla ice cream over crust. Spread sherbet over ice cream. Spread remaining ice cream over sherbet. Sprinkle reserved crumbs over top. Cover and freeze. Makes 6 servings.

Vanilla Mocha Pie

1¾   **cups chocolate wafer cookie crumbs**
¼   **cup butter, melted**
1   **pint vanilla ice cream, softened**
1   **pint coffee ice cream, softened**
1   **to 2 toffee candy bars, crushed**

Combine cookie crumbs and butter. Press into the bottom and sides of a 9-inch pie pan. Bake 5 minutes and let cool on rack.

Spread vanilla ice cream over crust; place in freezer until firm. Spread coffee ice cream over top; sprinkle with crushed toffee bars. Freeze, then cover until ready to serve. It may be necessary to stand at room temperature a few minutes before cutting. Makes 6 servings.

Freeze

This yummy recipe reminds me of my childhood, when a Dreamsicle ice cream bar was so good on a hot summer day.

Oven 350°F
Freeze

Variation:
Use assorted ice cream flavors and toppings.

Apple Pie Delight

Oven 350°F

This is apple pie without the crust. Very rich and should be served in small portions. If desired, serve with a small scoop of vanilla ice cream.

1   cup flour
2   cups sugar, divided
½   cup chilled butter, cut into small pieces
2   tablespoons cornstarch
5   cups coarsely chopped apples

Combine the flour and 1 cup sugar, then cut in the butter until the pieces are pea size. Press half the mixture onto bottom of a sprayed 8x8-inch baking dish. Top with apples.

In a medium saucepan, combine remaining 1 cup sugar and the cornstarch. Add *1 cup water* and cook, stirring frequently, until thickened. Pour over apples and sprinkle with remaining crumb mixture. Bake about 1 hour and 20 minutes or until apples are tender and topping has browned. Serve warm. Makes 9 servings.

Rustic Pear Pie

Oven 400°F

Variation: Substitute apples or peaches for the pears.

1   (10-inch) unbaked pie crust
4   medium fairly ripe pears, peeled, cored, sliced
½   cup sugar
3   tablespoons flour
1   tablespoon sliced almonds

Place pie crust loosely in a deep 10-inch pie dish.

In a mixing bowl, toss the pears with the sugar and flour. Spoon into the center of the pie crust, mounding the pears and leaving about a 1-inch border from the edge of the dish. Bring the crust up and over the pears, crimping the folds lightly. Not all the pears will be covered. Cover with foil and bake 15 to 20 minutes or until pears are tender. Remove foil and sprinkle with almonds the last 5 minutes of baking time. Serve warm or room temperature. Makes 6 servings.

Rustic Pies

Rustic pies are quite the rage right now and can best be described as a pie baked without a pie dish. It doesn't work with runny type pies or cream pies, but it is great made with apples, peaches and pears. The pie dough is placed on a baking sheet and the center is filled with sweetened fruit, leaving a 2-inch border from the edge of the dough. The dough is brought up and over and crimped slightly on the folds. The center of the fruit should be showing. It is then baked on the baking sheet.

This is a great way to make a pie, but most of the time I prefer doing it in a deep dish pie dish. This is easier and keeps its shape better. Just place the crust lightly in the pie dish, mound the fruit in the center leaving a border, and bring the pie dough up to partially cover the fruit; then crimp the folds lightly. Very easy and it makes beautiful pies.

Rustic Apple Pie

Oven 400°F

1	(10-inch) unbaked pie crust
8	cups sliced apples (Braeburns are good)
1	cup sugar, divided
1	teaspoon cinnamon
¾	cup flour
⅓	cup butter

Dazzle your friends with this wonderful dessert. Serve each slice with a sprinkle of powdered sugar and they will be even more impressed.

Place pie crust loosely in a deep 10-inch pie dish, but do not shape. Fill crust with apples. Combine ½ cup sugar and cinnamon and sprinkle over apples.

Combine remaining ½ cup sugar with the flour. With a pastry blender or fork, cut in butter until crumbly, but not fine. Sprinkle over apples. Bring crust up and over the apples, crimping the folds lightly. Not all the apples will be covered. Cover pie with foil and bake 25 minutes. Remove foil and bake about 30 minutes or until apples are tender. Watch carefully toward the end and cover with foil again, if necessary, to prevent burning. Let cool on rack. Makes 6 to 8 servings.

Perfect Pie Crust

This really is a reliable recipe. The dough can be refrigerated up to 3 days or can be frozen. You may not always need this large a recipe, but any left over can be formed into balls and frozen or better yet, roll out to desired size, place on a baking sheet and freeze. Then wrap and freeze until ready to use.

4	cups flour
1	tablespoon sugar
2	teaspoons salt
1¾	cups shortening (do not substitute)
1	tablespoon cider or white vinegar
1	large egg

Combine flour, sugar and salt in a mixing bowl. Cut in shortening with two knives or a pastry blender. Combine vinegar and egg with *½ cup cold water*; add to flour mixture. Stir until moistened and a dough is formed. Divide dough into 4 equal parts; shape each into a round flat patty ready for rolling. Wrap in waxed paper; chill at least 30 minutes.

When ready to use, place on lightly floured board; roll ⅛-inch thick and 2 inches larger than inverted pie pan. Makes 4 single crusts.

Graham Cracker Crust

Oven 350°F

I know it is more convenient to buy a graham cracker crust, but if time permits, do try this recipe. You will be surprised at how much better it is and how much money you will save.

1¼	cups graham cracker crumbs
¼	cup sugar
⅓	cup butter, melted

Combine ingredients and press into bottom and sides of 9-inch pie pan. Bake 10 minutes. Cool.

Pretzel Pie Crust

¾	cup butter, melted
2⅔	cups crushed pretzels
3	tablespoons sugar

Combine ingredients and pat into two 9-inch pie pans or one 13x9-inch pan. Bake 10 minutes. Cool.

Pie Crust

2½	cups flour
½	teaspoon salt
¾	cup shortening
6	to 7 tablespoons ice water

Combine flour and salt in a mixing bowl. With two knives or a pastry blender, cut in shortening until uniform, about the size of peas. Sprinkle with water, a tablespoon at a time, and toss with fork. Stir gently, just until dough forms a ball. Divide into 2 equal parts; place on lightly floured surface and roll to ⅛-inch thickness. Gently ease into pan to avoid stretching. Makes 2 single crusts.

Oven 350°F

This makes a great crust for ice cream or the Key Lime Pie on page 72.

Always

Always

Always

Read through a recipe before you begin.

An Apple a Day

You may have additional varieties in your area,
but this is a good starting point.

Braeburn	Excellent all purpose apple. Good for eating out of hand or for cooking and baking. Also keeps well.
Cortland	A slightly tart versatile apple. Good for baking.
Elstar	A sweet-tart flavor; versatile. Good for snacks, salad and baking.
Empire	Best for snacks and salads than for cooking.
Fuji	Good eating apple; sweet, crunchy and flavorful. A good choice for pies.
Gala	Good eating and baking apple.
Golden Delicious	Good eating apple. Perfect for sautéing and baking in casseroles. Great for applesauce and pies.
Granny Smith	Tart and firm apple. A favorite for pies.
Jonagold	Good all around eating, cooking and baking apple.
Jonathon	All-purpose. Good for cooking and baking. Really a good versatile apple.
McIntosh	Sweet-tart flavor. Good for sauces, but not for pies because it loses its shape once cooked.
Red Delicious	A good eating apple, nice for salads.
Rome	Not a favorite for eating. Good for pies, breads, sauce, bread pudding and baking whole.

Cookies & Candies

Easy Sugar Cookies

½   cup butter, softened
½   cup sugar, plus some to sprinkle on top
1   teaspoon vanilla extract
1   large egg yolk (reserve white)
1   cup flour

Combine ingredients in mixer bowl until blended. Shape into small balls and place on ungreased cookie sheet.

Beat egg white slightly with fork. Dip fork in egg white and lightly press cookie. Sprinkle with additional sugar. Bake 8 to 10 minutes. They should not brown but should be light in color. Makes 2½ dozen.

Oven 350°F

Kids also enjoy making these quick and easy cookies.

Sugar Cookie Kisses

1¼   cups sugar, divided
¾   cup butter, softened
1   egg
1¾   cups flour
1   teaspoon baking soda
48   candy kisses

Cream 1 cup of the sugar and the butter in a mixer bowl. Add egg and beat until well mixed.

Combine flour and baking soda. Add to creamed mixture, beating until thoroughly mixed. Cover and chill at least 1 hour or until firm.

Shape dough into 1-inch balls and roll in remaining sugar. Place on ungreased baking sheets and bake 8 to 10 minutes or until lightly browned.

Remove from oven and immediately press a candy kiss in center of each cookie. Remove and cool on rack. Makes about 4 dozen.

Chill
Oven 375°F

Candy kisses aren't just chocolate anymore. Try a different flavor each time. Some have nuts, some have toffee and some are mixed white and milk chocolate.

Cookies... Real or Fake

Homemade cookies are so much better than store-bought. In fact, when offered a cookie, my grandson will ask his mom if it's "real" or "fake," meaning homemade or storebought.

With a family it's a good idea to make a double recipe and freeze some for school lunches. If you don't have time to bake them all, or if you prefer the fresh baked taste, you can drop spoonfuls onto wax paper-lined cookie sheets and freeze. When frozen, remove from sheet, place in a resealable plastic bag and store in freezer. Remove desired amount and bake.

Oven 350°F

Peanut Butter Drop Cookies

The basic cookie is very simple and delicious on its own, but if the mood strikes you, you can always add a few extra ingredients.

Note: This recipe does not contain flour!

1   cup peanut butter
1   cup sugar
1   large egg
1   teaspoon baking soda

In mixing bowl, combine all ingredients and mix until well blended. Form into walnut size balls and place on ungreased cookie sheet. Bake 12 to 15 minutes or until golden. They should be slightly soft in the center. Makes about 18 cookies.

Variation: Add chocolate chips and/or chopped nuts. Or, after removing from oven, top centers with chocolate chips, an M&M® candy or a chocolate kiss. YUM!

Makes-a-lot Brownies

6	eggs
1	cup vegetable oil
3	cups sugar
5	(1-oz) squares semi-sweet chocolate, melted
1½	cups flour
1	teaspoon baking powder

Brownies go fast, so you might as well make a whole bunch.

In a large bowl, combine eggs and oil until blended. Stir in the sugar. Add the melted chocolate.

Combine flour and baking powder and add to above mixture, stirring just until blended. Pour into a sprayed 17x12-inch sheet pan. Bake 20 to 30 minutes or until center tests done. Makes about 36 brownies.

Note: The pan I used is the kind usually found at discount warehouse stores. It is somewhat larger than a 15x10-inch jelly roll pan.

Peanut Butter Krispie Bars

Stove Top

¼	cup butter
40	large marshmallows
5	cups crispy rice cereal
¼	cup creamy peanut butter

This is a twist on an all time favorite recipe. You can melt the butter and marshmallows in the microwave if you prefer, but remember to stir frequently.

In a large saucepan, melt butter over low heat. Add marshmallows and cook, stirring constantly, until melted and smooth. Remove from heat and quickly stir in the peanut butter.

Add cereal and stir until well mixed. Spoon into a sprayed 13x9-inch baking dish and press evenly, using spatula or buttered hands - because mixture is hot. Cool and cut into squares. Makes about 24.

Pecan Shortbread Cookies

Everyone loves these little cookies. Put on the coffee pot and have friends over for coffee, cookies and great conversation.

Note: Cut cookies evenly by making 3 lengthwise cuts and five crosswise cuts. You should then have 24 squares. Then cut diagonally, cutting each square in half, to yield 48 cookies.

1¼	cups butter, softened
1¾	cups powdered sugar, divided
3	cups flour
1	cup chopped pecans, divided
1	lemon (2 tablespoons juice, 1 teaspoon peel)

In a large mixer bowl, combine butter and ¾ cup of the powdered sugar and beat until light and fluffy. Add flour and beat just until blended. Stir in ½ cup of the pecans. Press dough into an ungreased 15x10-inch baking pan. Sprinkle with remaining ½ cup pecans and bake 20 to 25 minutes or until light golden – watch carefully. Place pan on wire rack and while hot, cut into squares and then cut each square diagonally in half. Let cool in pan.

Combine remaining 1 cup powdered sugar with lemon peel and just enough lemon juice to make a glaze. Drizzle cookies with the glaze; let set slightly, then remove from pan. Makes 48 cookies.

Be Prepared and Save Time

When making cookies, try to allow time to make a double batch. If making bar cookies, assemble in pan, cover and freeze. If making a drop cookie; shape into 1 or 2 logs, wrap tightly and freeze. When ready to use, just slice and bake. This can be a life-saver when the kids show up with a group of hungry friends.

Chocolate Walnut Brownies

1	cup butter
1⅔	cups semi-sweet chocolate chips, divided
2	cups sugar
3	large eggs
1	cup flour
1	cup coarsely chopped walnuts

Melt butter and ⅔ cup of the chocolate chips over very low heat. Remove from heat. Stir in sugar. Add eggs; stir until well mixed. Add flour and nuts.

Pour into a sprayed 13x9-inch baking pan. Sprinkle with remaining 1 cup chocolate chips. Bake 30 to 35 minutes or until tester inserted in center comes out almost clean (do not over bake). Cool. Makes about 24.

Stove Top
Oven 350°F

When I made these brownies, while camping or boating, I was amazed at how many "new" friends showed up. Kids and adults!

Raisin Crunchies

2	cups semi-sweet chocolate chips
½	teaspoon vanilla extract
1½	cups raisins
½	cup peanuts
1	cup corn flakes

Melt chocolate chips in top of double boiler, stirring until smooth. Remove from heat; stir in vanilla, raisins, peanuts and cereal. Drop by teaspoon onto wax paper lined cookie sheet. Chill until firm. Makes about 3½ dozen.

Stove Top
Chill

Tip: If desired, spread mixture into a lightly buttered 8x8-inch dish. Chill before cutting into squares.

I try to always have a cake mix on hand to make these quick and easy chocolate cookies.

Chocolate Nut Bars

1	(18.25-oz) box Devil's Food cake mix
2	large eggs
½	cup butter, melted
1	cup semi-sweet chocolate chips
1	cup chopped walnuts or pecans, divided

Combine first 3 ingredients in mixing bowl, stirring until all dry ingredients are moistened. Add chocolate chips and ¾ cup of the nuts. Press into a sprayed 13x9-inch baking pan. Sprinkle with remaining ¼ cup nuts.

Bake 20 to 25 minutes or until tester inserted in center comes out clean. Cool and cut into bars. Makes 30 bars.

When my children were small we did a lot of camping and, of course, a lot of eating. We often joined other large families. Anyway, needless to say, we went through a lot of healthy, good for you food, but also a lot of desserts and cookies. We sometimes went through two batches of brownies a day - we just couldn't keep the adults away from them.

Patrick's Favorite Brownies

1	cup butter, softened
2	cups sugar
3	squares (1-oz each) unsweetened chocolate, melted
4	large eggs
1½	cups flour

In mixer bowl, cream butter and sugar thoroughly. Add melted chocolate, then eggs. Stir in the flour.

Pour into a sprayed 13x9-inch pan and bake 25 minutes or until tester inserted in center comes out clean. Do not over bake. Cool and cut into squares. Makes about 30 brownies.

Mosaic Cookies

2	cups semi-sweet chocolate chips
1/2	cup butter
1	(10½-oz) package colored miniature marshmallows
1	cup chopped walnuts
3½	cups flaked coconut

In top of double boiler, melt the chocolate chips and butter. Place marshmallows and nuts in a large mixing bowl. Pour melted chocolate over top; stir carefully to coat. Chill about 15 minutes for easier handling.

Sprinkle coconut on bread board. Spoon one third of chocolate mixture in a long row (about 10 to 12 inches) on top of coconut. Roll in coconut, shaping to make about a 12-inch roll. Place on waxed paper or foil; wrap and twist ends. Repeat with remaining mixture. Chill until firm. Slice to serve. Makes about 7 dozen.

Stove Top, Chill

This is one of our favorite holiday cookies. I had to hide them in the freezer or my children would have eaten all of them before Christmas.

Christmas Holly Cookies

35	large marshmallows
1/2	cup butter
1	teaspoon vanilla extract
1½	teaspoons green food coloring (approx.)
4	cups corn flakes
	Red hot candies (for decoration)

Melt marshmallows and butter in top of double boiler; stir to blend. Stir in vanilla extract and enough food coloring to make a dark green. Remove from heat and gently stir in cereal.

Working quickly, drop by teaspoon onto wax paper-lined cookie sheet. Decorate each cookie with 3 red hots for holly berries. Chill. Makes 3 dozen.

Stove Top, Chill

These make a colorful addition to a tray of assorted holiday cookies.

Chocolate Coconut Bars

1½	cups graham cracker crumbs
½	cup butter, melted
2⅓	cups flaked coconut
1	(14-oz) can sweetened condensed milk
2	cups semi-sweet chocolate chips
½	cup creamy peanut butter

Combine graham cracker crumbs and melted butter. Press into ungreased 13x9-inch baking dish. Sprinkle coconut over top. Pour condensed milk over coconut. Bake 25 to 30 minutes or until lightly browned.

Meanwhile, over low heat, melt chocolate chips with peanut butter. Pour over hot coconut layer. Let cool. Cut into bars. Makes about 30 cookies.

Layered Chocolate Bars

1	(18-oz) package sugar cookie dough, softened
2	cups semi-sweet chocolate chips
2	cups flaked coconut
1	cup pecans
1	(4-oz) can sweetened condensed milk

Pat cookie dough evenly into a lightly sprayed 15x10-inch baking pan. Sprinkle with the chocolate chips, coconut and then the pecans. Pour condensed milk over the top. Bake 20 to 22 minutes or until lightly browned and center is set. Makes 45 cookies.

Butter Pecan Cookies

Bake 325°F

1	cup butter, softened
¾	cup sugar
½	teaspoon baking soda
½	teaspoon white vinegar
1½	cups flour
¾	cup chopped pecans, toasted

In mixer bowl, beat butter about 1 minute. Add sugar, baking soda and vinegar and beat 7 to 8 minutes or until fluffy and turns almost white in color. By hand, stir in the flour and then the pecans. Drop onto an ungreased baking sheet making mounds slightly smaller than a walnut. Bake 18 to 20 minutes or until lightly browned around the edges. Makes 3 dozen cookies.

These are simple ingredients that turn into a very crisp butter flavored cookie. Delicious served with a glass of milk or your favorite ice cream.

Peanut Butter Cookies

Bake 350°F

½	cup butter, softened
1	cup packed light brown sugar
1½	cups chunky peanut butter
1	large egg
1¾	cup flour
1	teaspoon baking powder

Combine butter, brown sugar and peanut butter in a mixer bowl, beating until light in color. Add the egg and mix well. Combine flour and baking powder and mix just until flour is blended. Make walnut-size balls and place on ungreased baking sheets. Flatten with a fork in a crisscross pattern. Bake 10 to 12 minutes. Cookies should be slightly soft in the center. Makes about 36 cookies.

Is there anyone who doesn't like peanut butter cookies? Let the kids make these for their school lunches or after school snacks.

After School Chocolate Cookies

Keep a cake mix on hand to make these "kid favorite" cookies.

1	(18.25-oz) box Milk Chocolate cake mix
½	cup oatmeal
½	cup vegetable oil
2	large eggs
½	cup raisins
1	cup semi-sweet chocolate chips

In mixer bowl, beat cake mix, oatmeal, oil and eggs just until blended. Stir in raisins and chocolate chips. The dough will be stiff.

Form into balls slightly smaller than a walnut and press slightly to flatten. Place about 2 inches apart on an ungreased cookie sheet. Bake 10 to 12 minutes. Cookies should still be soft in the center. Makes about 4 dozen cookies.

Chocolate Chow Mein Cookies

Stove Top
Chill

Another kids' favorite. They also make a nice addition to a holiday cookie tray.

1	cup butterscotch chips
1	cup semi-sweet chocolate chips
1	cup chopped walnuts
1	(5-oz) can Chow Mein noodles

Melt chips in top of double boiler; stir until blended and smooth. Remove from heat. Add walnuts and Chow Mein noodles; gently stir until evenly coated. Drop by teaspoon onto wax paper-lined cookie sheet. Chill until firm. Store in refrigerator. Makes about 5 dozen.

Bar Cookies

Bar cookies are sometimes hard to remove from the pan and still maintain nice smooth edges. It helps if you line the pan with foil, extending the foil over the ends of the pan. Spray lightly with cooking spray, then fill with cookie or candy mixture. When ready to cut, remove from pan, peel off the foil and cut.

Coconut Nut Bars

Oven 350°F

¼	cup butter, melted
1½	cups quick-cooking oats
1½	cups flaked coconut
1	(14-oz) can sweetened condensed milk
1	cup semi-sweet chocolate chips
½	cup chopped pecans or walnuts

You can play around with this recipe by using a variety of chips and nuts.

Pour butter into a 13x9-inch baking dish. Sprinkle oats evenly over butter (most of the oats will not be coated). Sprinkle coconut over the top. Pour condensed milk over coconut. Sprinkle with chocolate chips and pecans. Press down slightly.

Bake 20 to 25 minutes or until just lightly browned. Cool before cutting into bars. Makes 30 bars.

Quick Chocolate Bars

1	(18.25-oz) box white cake mix
⅓	cup vegetable oil
2	large eggs
¼	cup butter
1	(14-oz) can sweetened condensed milk
1	cup semi-sweet chocolate chips

In a medium bowl, combine first three ingredients. Mix thoroughly with a stiff spatula or wooden spoon. Press two-thirds of the mixture into a sprayed 13x9-inch baking pan.

In small saucepan, melt butter over low heat. Add condensed milk and chocolate chips. Cook until mixture is melted, stirring until smooth. Pour evenly over crust. By hand, drop small pieces of dough over top. Bake 25 to 30 minutes or until lightly browned and chocolate filling feels somewhat firm. Cool and cut into bars. Makes 40 bars.

Butterscotch Drop Cookies

2	cups butterscotch chips
½	cup creamy or chunky peanut butter
2	cups corn flakes

Melt butterscotch chips and peanut butter in top of double boiler. Remove from heat and gently stir in corn flakes to coat. Drop by teaspoon on wax paper-lined cookie sheet. Chill until set. Makes 3½ dozen.

Stove Top
Oven 350°F

Remember the Chocolate Revel Bars that are so popular and get gobbled up almost as soon as they come out of the oven? Well, these are just about as good and a whole lot easier to make.

Stove Top
Chill

With these pantry items, you can always make these cookies at a moments notice.

Mom's Peanut Butter Cookies

Oven 350°F

1	cup peanut butter, smooth or crunchy
1	cup sugar
1	large egg
1	teaspoon vanilla extract
¼	cup semi-sweet chocolate chips
¼	cup chopped walnuts

Combine ingredients and mix well. Drop by teaspoon onto ungreased baking sheet. Bake 6 to 8 minutes or until the cookies are slightly soft in the center and lightly browned. Makes about 2½ dozen.

This is an unusual cookie because it doesn't have any flour in the recipe.

Peanut Butter Oatmeal Bars

Oven 350°F
Stove Top,
Chill

⅔	cup butter, melted
¼	cup, plus ⅓ cup creamy peanut butter
¼	cup light corn syrup
1	cup firmly packed light brown sugar
4	cups quick-cooking oatmeal
1½	cups semi-sweet chocolate chips

In mixing bowl, combine butter, ¼ cup peanut butter, corn syrup, brown sugar and oatmeal. Press evenly into a sprayed 13x9-inch baking pan. Bake 10 to 12 minutes or until just starting to brown around the edges. Don't over bake or you won't be able to cut into nice neat bars. Place on rack and let cool while preparing frosting.

In a small saucepan, melt chocolate chips and the ⅓ cup peanut butter; stir to blend. Spread over cookie mixture and let cool. Cover and store in refrigerator until frosting is set. Makes about 30 bars.

A great lunch box cookie. Just wrap in a little plastic wrap and pack.

Lemon Nut Cookies

Add this delicious cookie to your list of family favorite cookie recipes.

1	(18.25-oz) box lemon cake mix
2	large eggs
½	cup vegetable oil
1½	teaspoons fresh lemon peel
⅓	cup finely chopped walnuts

In large mixer bowl, combine first four ingredients. Beat on low until thoroughly mixed. Drop rounded teaspoons about 2 inches apart onto ungreased cookie sheets. They should be slightly smaller than a walnut.

With finger, make an indentation in middle of each cookie, pressing almost to the bottom. Fill with chopped nuts. Bake 9 to 12 minutes. Cookies should not brown, but will flatten slightly just before the cookies test done. Makes 48 cookies.

Cookie Tips

- Have eggs and butter at room temperature.

- Measure accurately using glass measuring cups for liquid and dry measuring cups for dry ingredients.

- Avoid using dark cookie sheets. They will absorb more heat and can cause over browning.

- Grease cookie sheets and baking dishes only if instructed to do so.

- Bake cookies on medium rack.

- Cool cookies on a baking rack.

- Always cool baking sheet before cooking a new batch.

Chocolate Peanut Squares

½	cup butter, melted
5½	double graham crackers, crushed fine
2	cups sifted powdered sugar
½	cup chunky peanut butter
1	cup semi-sweet chocolate chips

Pour melted butter over graham cracker crumbs, stirring to blend. Add powdered sugar and peanut butter; mix well. Pat into sprayed 8x8-inch pan, spreading evenly.

Melt chocolate chips in top of double boiler. Spread over top of mixture. Chill until firm, but not hard, about 30 minutes. Cut into squares. Cover and chill until ready to serve. Makes 25 squares.

Stove Top Chill

Delicious! Those yummy Peanut Butter Cups have some competition here. These freeze well.

Walnut Shortbread

2	cups butter, softened
1	cup sugar
1	cup walnuts, finely ground
2	teaspoons vanilla extract
4	cups flour

In large mixer bowl, cream the butter and sugar until light and fluffy. Add walnuts, vanilla and flour and beat just until mixed. Spoon into a sprayed 15x10-inch jelly roll pan and spread evenly.

Bake 30 to 40 minutes or until light and golden. Cool and cut into small bars or squares. Makes about 48 cookies.

Oven 325°F

Shortbread can be addictive; you keep going back for more. This is a large recipe, but it will keep for several days if tightly covered.

Quick Chocolate Cookies

Oven 350ºF

My grandson Ben loves to make these cookies. They are quick and easy for him to make and he takes pride in making a delicious cookie that everyone enjoys.

1	(18.25-oz) box German Chocolate cake mix
½	cup vegetable oil
2	large eggs
½	cup flaked coconut
1	cup chopped walnuts or pecans

In a mixer bowl, beat the cake mix, oil, and eggs until blended. Add coconut and nuts and beat on low just until mixed. Drop dough by rounded teaspoons (less than walnut size), onto an ungreased baking sheet. Bake 12 to 14 minutes. Cookies should be slightly soft in the center. Makes about 4 dozen cookies.

Cranberry–Nut Shortbread Cookies

Oven 325ºF

A wonderful, not too sweet, shortbread cookie.

1¼	cups butter, softened
1	cup sifted powdered sugar
2¼	cups flour
½	cup dried cranberries
½	cup chopped pecans or hazelnuts

In mixer bowl, cream the butter and sugar. Gradually add the flour and beat just until mixed. Stir in the cranberries and nuts.

Form into 1-inch balls and place on an ungreased baking sheet. Spray the bottom of a small glass, dip in sugar and flatten each ball to a little more than ¼-inch thick. Bake 12 to 14 minutes or until just the bottoms are golden. Makes about 48 cookies.

Snowballs

1	cup semi-sweet chocolate chips
1/3	cup canned evaporated milk
1	cup sifted powdered sugar
1/2	cup finely chopped walnuts
1¼	cups flaked coconut

Combine chocolate chips and milk in top of double boiler. Heat until melted, stirring to blend. Remove from heat. Stir in powdered sugar and walnuts. Chill slightly (until mixture just begins to hold its shape).

Drop by teaspoon onto mound of coconut. Roll in coconut; form into balls. Chill until set. Makes 2½ to 3 dozen.

White Chocolate Clusters

12	ounces white chocolate
3	cups coarsely chopped pecans or walnuts
1/3	cup semi-sweet chocolate chips

Melt white chocolate in top of double boiler or in a heavy saucepan over very low heat. Remove from heat and add pecans. Gently stir in the chocolate chips.

Drop by tablespoon onto wax paper; cool. Makes about 48 candies.

Variation: Omit chocolate chips and add dried cranberries, blueberries or other dried fruit.

Stove Top Chill

Snowballs are a must for the holidays. We have been enjoying this recipe for over thirty years. Buy coconut when it is on sale and double or triple the recipe. They can be made several months ahead and frozen.

Stove Top

Real white chocolate (as opposed to almond bark) has a very low melting point. If allowed to get too hot, it will be grainy and sometimes almost crunchy. If this happens, don't try to revive it, you'll have no choice but to throw it away. This is expensive, so remember... Low Heat.

Microwave Peanut Brittle

1	cup sugar
½	cup light corn syrup
1¾	cup Spanish peanuts
1	teaspoon butter
1	teaspoon vanilla extract
1	teaspoon baking soda

In a 4-cup glass measuring cup (or microwave safe bowl), combine sugar and corn syrup. Cook on high 4 minutes. Add peanuts and cook 4 minutes. Add butter and vanilla; cook 1 minute. Quickly fold in baking soda. Quickly spread on greased cookie sheet to cool. Break into pieces.

Variation:
Use cashews or dry roasted peanuts. Mixed nuts are also very good. Cooking time may vary according to wattage of individual microwave ovens.

Stove Top
Chill

Just a tiny bit of dried cranberries adds color as well as flavor.

Cran–Pecan Chocolate Bark

12	ounces milk chocolate
1	tablespoon shortening
¼	cup dried cranberries
¾	cup finely chopped pecans

In small heavy saucepan, melt chocolate and shortening over very low heat. Remove from heat and stir in cranberries and ¼ cup pecans.

Pour into a buttered, then wax paper lined 11x7-inch baking dish; spread evenly. Sprinkle with remaining pecans; press lightly. Chill about 45 minutes to set. Remove and break into small pieces. Makes 24 candies.

Eggs & Brunch

Baked Bacon Omelet

6	large eggs, lightly beaten
⅓	cup Half & Half
3	slices bacon, cooked, crumbled
¼	teaspoon pepper
1½	cups (6-oz) Cheddar cheese, shredded
¼	cup chopped green onion

Combine eggs, Half & Half, and ⅓ *cup water*. Add bacon, pepper, cheese, and onion. Pour into a sprayed 8x8-inch baking dish. Bake 18 to 20 minutes or until center is set. Makes 4 to 6 servings.

Oven 400°F

Have cooked bacon on hand in the freezer for these tasty omelets.

Tip: Omelets are easier to make if cooked in a curve-sided nonstick skillet.

Ham & Cheese Omelet

1	tablespoon butter
1	tablespoon diced apple
2	large eggs
⅓	cup diced ham
¼	cup (1-oz) Swiss cheese, shredded

Melt butter in a 9-inch nonstick skillet. Add apple and cook until just tender. Remove apple and set aside.

Combine eggs with *1 tablespoon water*. Add to skillet and cook until eggs begin to set. Then gently lift edges to allow egg to flow underneath. When eggs are lightly set, spoon apple, ham, and cheese over one side. Let cook about 1 minute. Fold in half and serve. Makes 1 serving.

Stove Top

I added a little apple here, not much, just 1 tablespoon, but what a treat!

Sausage Egg Scramble

4	ounces sausage
¼	cup chopped onion
2	tablespoons chopped green pepper
6	large eggs
½	cup (2-oz) Pepper Jack cheese, shredded

Cook sausage, onion, and green pepper in a medium skillet; drain.

Combine eggs with ¼ *cup water*. Add to sausage and cook over medium heat, stirring occasionally. Sprinkle with cheese and serve. Makes 4 servings.

Ham & Cheese Bake

3	cups frozen hash browns, thawed
1	cup (4-oz) Swiss cheese, shredded
1	cup finely diced ham
1	cup (4-oz) Pepper Jack cheese, shredded
4	large eggs, lightly beaten
1	cup Half & Half

Place hash browns in a sprayed 1½-quart deep casserole. Bake 20 minutes. Remove from oven and reduce temperature to 350°F. Sprinkle Swiss cheese over potatoes, then ham and then the Monterey Jack cheese.

In a small mixing bowl combine the eggs and Half & Half. Pour over the cheese. Bake, uncovered, about 45 minutes or until center is set. Makes 4 servings.

Note: It is sometimes hard to tell exactly when the center is set in this recipe. A knife inserted in the center should look fairly dry. The casserole will continue to cook somewhat if allowed to stand about 10 minutes. This is also good reheated.

Ham and Egg Scramble

1	tablespoon butter
2	tablespoons chopped onion
¼	cup chopped fresh mushrooms
½	cup diced ham
4	large eggs, lightly beaten
	Salt and pepper, to taste

Melt butter in a medium skillet. Add onion and cook until almost soft. Add mushrooms and cook through. Stir in the ham.

Add eggs, salt, and pepper. Cook, stirring frequently, until almost set. Makes 2 servings.

Stove Top

An easy way to use up that last little bit of ham. Or, use bacon or pepperoni.

Swiss Strata

1	loaf (8-oz) French bread
1	cup ham, cubed or cut into slices
1	cup (4-oz) Swiss cheese, shredded
6	large eggs, lightly beaten
1	cup whipping cream or Half and Half
1	cup milk

Tear bread into chunks and place in a sprayed 13x9-inch baking dish. Sprinkle with ham and cheese.

In medium mixing bowl, combine the eggs, whipping cream, and milk. Pour over bread mixture. Cover and refrigerate overnight. Bake, uncovered, 40 to 45 minutes, or until golden. Makes 8 servings.

Chill
Oven 350°F

Being able to prepare a dish the night before and bake the next day is right up there with slow-cooking for me. It makes a company breakfast or brunch so much easier. Just add fresh fruit, coffee, and juice.

Hint: If you are unable to find an 8-oz loaf of bread, purchase a 16-oz loaf and use the other half for dinner or French toast.

Bacon Breakfast Pizza

A deliciously quick and easy pizza for breakfast, lunch or dinner.

Hint: This doesn't reheat well, so enjoy the first time around.

1	(13.8-oz) can refrigerated pizza dough
6	large eggs, scrambled, but still moist
2	tablespoons finely chopped onion
3	tablespoons finely chopped green pepper
8	slices bacon, cooked and crumbled
1	cup (4-oz) Cheddar cheese, shredded

Unroll pizza dough and pat evenly onto a sprayed 12-inch pizza pan, forming a rim around the edges. Spoon the scrambled eggs over the crust. Sprinkle with onion, green pepper and then the bacon. Sprinkle cheese evenly over the top. Bake 8 to 10 minutes or until crust is lightly browned. Makes 4 to 6 servings.

Casserole or Baking Dish...

Do you know the difference?

A CASSEROLE DISH is usually a round, square or oval deep dish and is referred to in quart sizes such as a 2-quart casserole dish.

A BAKING DISH is usually a rectangle, square or oval shallow dish no more than 2-2½ inches deep. They are usually referred to in measurements such as a 13x9-inch baking dish or pan.

Cinnamon Sugar Oatmeal

2	cups quick oats (1 minute type)
2	tablespoons sugar
½	teaspoon cinnamon
⅔	cup Half & Half
	Butter
	Brown sugar

In a medium saucepan, bring *2½ cups water* to a boil. Stirring constantly, gradually add the oatmeal. Add sugar and cinnamon; mix well. Cook 1 minute.

Add Half & Half and bring to a boil. Pour into individual serving dishes. Top each with a dab of butter and a sprinkle of brown sugar. Makes 6 servings.

Stove Top

Tip: If desired, substitute whole milk or 2% for the Half & Half.

Broccoli–Ham Quiche

3	large eggs, lightly beaten
1	cup heavy cream
1	cup small broccoli florets
½	cup cubed ham
½	cup (2-oz) Gruyère cheese, shredded

Combine eggs and cream. Add remaining ingredients and pour into a sprayed 9-inch pie dish. Bake 20 to 25 minutes or until center is set. Makes 6 servings.

Oven 375°F

If you need just a small amount of ham, buy a ¼-inch slice of deli ham.

Why Not?

Quiche for dinner? Why not?

It contains protein, carbohydrates, vegetables and dairy. Plus it's easy. Serve with fresh or canned fruit and dinner is ready in a jif.

Company Maple Sausages

16	pork sausage links
½	cup brown sugar
1	cup maple syrup

In a large skillet, brown sausages; drain off fat.

Combine brown sugar and maple syrup; pour over sausages. Bring to a boil, reduce heat, and simmer until sausages are glazed and mixture has thickened. Makes 4 to 5 servings.

Oven
Stove Top

Sausage patties and maple syrup sounds a little weird, but that's how some kids like them.

Variation:
Serve sausage patties topped with maple syrup. Add scrambled eggs and biscuits.

Sausage Biscuits

1	(10.2-oz) can of 5 jumbo size biscuits
5	sausage patties
5	slices Cheddar or American cheese
	Maple syrup (optional)

Bake biscuits according to package directions.

Meanwhile cook sausage; drain.

Cut biscuits in half horizontally. Place a sausage patty on each biscuit half; then a slice of cheese and top with the other biscuit half. Serve with Maple syrup, if desired. Makes 5 servings.

Variation: Serve sausage patties topped with maple syrup. Add scrambled eggs and biscuits.

Oven Pancake

Oven 425°F

½   cup flour
½   cup milk
2   large eggs
3   tablespoons butter
    Maple syrup

Combine flour and milk in a small mixing bowl, mixing with fork just until blended (batter will still be lumpy). Stir in eggs.

Place butter in a 9-inch pie pan and place in oven to melt.

Remove from oven; pour in batter. Bake 15 minutes or until puffed and golden. Serve immediately. Pancake will puff up, but will fall shortly after removing from oven. Makes 1 to 2 servings.

If you haven't had these pancakes before, you are in for a treat. They make a great breakfast or light dinner. Serve with fruit and bacon or sausage links or fill with peach slices, drizzle with maple syrup, and sprinkle with powdered sugar.

Oven French Toast

Oven 350°F

⅔   cup firmly packed brown sugar
½   cup butter, melted
1½   teaspoons cinnamon
6   large eggs, lightly beaten
1¾   cups milk
1   (1-lb) loaf French bread, cut into 1-inch slices

Combine the brown sugar, butter and cinnamon and spread evenly in a 15x10-inch baking pan.

Combine eggs and milk in a 13x9-inch dish. Add bread slices and soak for 2 to 3 minutes. Place bread in baking pan. Bake 25 to 30 minutes or until golden. Makes 6 servings.

This is a must have recipe when you have a hungry family to feed and not a lot of time.
If desired, sprinkle with powdered sugar and top with your favorite syrup or sliced peaches.

Pancake Mix

This mix is convenient to have on hand and much cheaper than store bought.

7½	cups flour
¼	cup baking powder
1	tablespoon, plus 1 teaspoon salt
⅔	cup sugar

Combine ingredients in a large bowl. Stir to mix thoroughly. Store in an airtight container at room temperature. Makes about 8½ cups mix.

Stove Top

Pancakes from "Pancake Mix"

1	large egg, lightly beaten
1	cup milk
2	tablespoons butter, melted
1¼	cups Pancake Mix

In mixing bowl, combine egg, milk, and butter. Add Pancake Mix and stir until dry ingredients are just moistened. Batter should be slightly lumpy. If batter seems a little thin, add more mix. For medium-large pancakes, use ¼ to ⅓ cup batter for each pancake and bake on a lightly oiled griddle or skillet, turning once, until golden brown.

Time Saver

Cook 1 to 2 pounds of bacon or sausage in the oven. Place in resealable plastic bags and freeze. Remove desired amount and microwave. This works great for busy school day mornings.

Soups, Sandwiches & Pizza

Chicken–Broccoli Soup

½   cup chopped onion
1   cup cubed cooked chicken
1   cup broccoli florets
1½   cups heavy cream
¼   teaspoon pepper
1½   cups (6-oz) Cheddar cheese, shredded

Place onion and ½ *cup water* in a large saucepan. Cook until tender.

Add chicken, broccoli, cream, pepper, and *1¼ cups water*. Bring to a boil, reduce heat, and cook until broccoli is tender. Gradually add cheese, stirring after each addition, until melted. Makes 6 cups.

Stove Top

A nice creamy cheese soup.

Chicken Noodle Soup

4   ounces linguine
7   cups chicken broth
1   small carrot, shredded
½   cup sliced celery
1   cup cubed, cooked chicken
¼   cup frozen peas

Break pasta into 2-inch lengths and cook according to package directions. Drain and rinse.

In a large pot, combine broth, carrots, and celery. Bring to a boil, reduce heat, and simmer until vegetables are tender, about 5 to 6 minutes. Add peas, chicken, and pasta. Cook until heated through. Makes 10 servings.

Stove Top

Our mom's were right…chicken soup is good for you.

Nothing warms the body like a hot bowl of soup on a cold winter night. For a complete meal, add a sandwich or salad and toasted bread or hot rolls.

Note: If you want to eliminate a good portion of the sodium, omit the seasoning packet that comes with the rice, you will still have plenty of flavor.

A light refreshing soup. Serve with toasted cheese sandwiches or a tossed green salad.

Cheesy Wild Rice Soup

1	(6-oz) box long-grain and wild rice mix
½	cup chopped onion
1½	cups chicken broth
2½	cups Half & Half
1	(10¾-oz) can Cream of Potato soup
2	cups (8-oz) Cheddar cheese, shredded

In medium saucepan, cook rice according to package directions; set aside.

Meanwhile, in a 3-quart saucepan, cook onion in a small amount of water until soft. Add chicken broth, Half & Half and soup. Heat, but do not boil (the cheese will curdle). Gradually add the cheese, stirring with each addition. Continue stirring until cheese is melted. Add the cooked rice. Makes 10 cups.

Chicken Pasta Soup

6	cups chicken broth
½	cup diced cooked chicken
3	ounces spaghetti broken into 1-inch pieces
½	cup green onion, 1-inch slices

Combine broth and chicken in a large saucepan. Bring to a boil; add spaghetti and cook about 7 minutes or until almost done.

Add onion and cook until pasta is tender. Makes 6 servings.

Chicken with Wild Rice Soup

Stove Top

1	(6-oz) package long-grain and wild rice mix
1	(10¾-oz) can condensed Cream of Potato soup.
4	cups milk
8	ounces process cheese spread, cubed
1½	cups cubed, cooked chicken

In a 3-quart saucepan or pot, prepare rice as directed on package.

Add soup and mix until blended. Add milk and cook until heated through. Gradually add cheese, stirring until melted. Add chicken and gently cook until heated through. Makes 9½ cups.

I tend to make this soup quite often, especially when I have leftover chicken or turkey. You can substitute Cheddar cheese, but remember to keep the heat low to prevent mixture from curdling.

Bean Soup & Sausage

Stove Top

1	(12-oz) package sausage
¾	cup chopped onion
1	(15-oz) can black beans, drained
1	(15-oz) can Great Northern beans, drained
1	(14.5-oz) can Diced Tomatoes with Basil, drained
1	(14.5-oz) can beef broth

In a large saucepan, brown sausage and onion; drain off fat. Rinse beans and add to pan along with tomatoes and broth. Bring to a boil, reduce heat, and simmer 15 minutes to blend flavor. Makes 6 cups.

Keep these ingredients on hand for a thick and hearty meal. Serve with toasted sourdough rolls and a fresh vegetable tray.

Company Egg Drop Soup

3	cups chicken broth
2	large eggs, beaten
⅓	cup chopped green onions
¾	cup sliced mushrooms
¼	cup chopped water chestnuts
1	tablespoon soy sauce

If desired, you can still make a delicious soup using just the first 3 ingredients.

In large saucepan, bring broth to a boil. Gradually add the eggs, stirring briskly after each addition.

Add remaining ingredients and cook until mushrooms are tender. Makes 4 cups.

Stove Top

Ground Beef Soup

1½	pounds lean ground beef
1	medium onion, chopped
2	cups cubed potatoes
1½	cups sliced carrots
1	(28-oz) can tomatoes, cut up
	Salt and pepper

To expand the recipe, you can add thinly sliced celery and any leftover vegetables such as peas and corn. My daughter saves time, by using tiny new potatoes, unpeeled and quartered. Serve with French bread.

Brown ground beef and onion; drain off fat.

Put meat mixture, potatoes, carrots, and tomatoes in a large stock pot. Add about *3 cups of water*. Cook 1 hour or until vegetables are tender. Add salt and pepper to taste. Makes 6 servings.

Tip: Regardless of what they say about freezing potatoes, this recipe can be frozen.

Vegetable Chowder

¾	cup chopped onion
2	cups peeled, cubed potatoes
1	(28-oz) can diced tomatoes
2	cups mixed vegetables
	Salt and pepper to taste

In a sprayed 3-quart saucepan or stock pot, cook onion until soft, but not brown. Add potatoes, tomatoes, and *3 cups water*. Bring to a boil, reduce heat, and simmer 15 minutes.

Add vegetables and cook 10 to 15 minutes or until potatoes are tender. Add salt and pepper to taste. Makes about 8 cups.

Note: Canned diced tomatoes are sometimes a larger dice than you may want for soup. They can be cut in the can by using kitchen shears or lightly pulsed in a blender or food processor.

Stove Top

A vegetable soup can become a heartier main dish by adding cooked ground beef, chicken, or leftover pot roast. If you like even more flavor, use seasoned canned tomatoes.

Sausage-Corn Chowder

12	ounces sausage
¾	cup chopped onion
1	(10¾-oz) can condensed Cream of Chicken Soup with Herbs
1¾	cup milk
1	(15-oz) can cream corn

In a large saucepan, cook sausage and onion, breaking sausage up into small pieces; drain off fat.

Combine soup and milk until smooth. Add to sausage, along with the corn. Cook until heated through. Makes 5½ cups.

Variation: If substituting ground beef or turkey, you may want to add additional seasoning or perhaps a can of Mexi-corn with its wonderful flavor of red and green peppers.

Stove Top

Lunch or dinner can be ready in less than 30 minutes. Just add bread and raw vegetables for a very satisfying meal.

Clam Chowder

1½	quarts chicken broth
2	cups finely chopped clams
2	cups small diced potatoes
½	cup small diced carrots
4	cups Half & Half
	Salt and pepper

Combine first 4 ingredients in large saucepan. Cook until vegetables are tender and mixture has thickened.

Stir in Half & Half. Add salt and pepper to taste. Makes 6 to 8 servings.

Chili Corn Soup

3	large potatoes, peeled and cubed (5 cups)
2½	cups frozen corn, thawed
2	(15-oz) cans chili with beans
4	cups beef broth

In large saucepan, cover potato cubes with water and boil until just tender, about 15 minutes; drain.

Meanwhile, place remaining ingredients in a large pot or Dutch oven. Add cooked potatoes. Bring mixture to a boil; reduce heat and simmer about 10 minutes to blend flavors. Makes about 10 cups.

This soup is so filling, all you really need is your choice of bread and perhaps a light dessert or fresh fruit to accompany it.

Baked Potato Soup

Stove Top

4	large baking potatoes, baked, then peeled and cubed
2	tablespoons butter
¾	cup finely chopped onion
2	tablespoons flour
2	cups Half & Half
	Salt and pepper to taste

As they do in restaurants, top with sour cream, cheese, chives and bacon just before serving.

Melt butter in large saucepan and cook onion and celery until tender.

Combine flour with ¼ cup of the Half & Half, mixing until smooth. Add to mixture in saucepan. Add *½ cup water*, salt and pepper. Bring mixture to a simmer, not a boil, and cook until heated through. Add the potatoes and then stir in the remaining Half & half. Continue cooking over low heat until hot, but do not boil. Makes 4 to 6 servings.

Beefy Salsa Chili

Stove Top

1	pound lean ground beef
1	cup chopped onion
1	(15-oz) can Chili Makins®
1	(14½-oz) can tomatoes, undrained
1	cup thick and chunky salsa
1	(15-oz) can black beans, drained

By adding a pound of ground beef to these pantry items, you have a family meal in less than 30 minutes.

In a large skillet, brown ground beef and onion; drain. Add remaining ingredients. Bring to a boil. Reduce heat and simmer 10 to 15 minutes to blend flavors and heat through. Makes 4 large servings.

Chili Bowl

A young mother, who didn't think she could cook, told me she made these for a special friend. She was thrilled that it was so easy and so attractive that she told another friend that she absolutely had to buy my books. More important, this encouraged her to venture out and try other recipes that she was reluctant to try before.

For each serving:
> **Small round loaf of bread, unsliced**
> **Melted butter**
> **Prepared or canned chili, heated**
> **Chopped onion**
> **Shredded Cheddar cheese**
> **Sour cream**

Cut a 1 to 1½-inch slice off the top of the bread. Remove three-fourths of bread from center forming a bowl. Brush inside with melted butter. Bake 6 minutes to lightly toast the bread. Remove from oven. Fill with hot chili. Sprinkle with onion and cheese. Top with sour cream. Makes 1 serving.

Chili Without the Beans

Stove Top

If desired, this recipe can be cooked in a slow cooker. Serve with cornbread and a fresh vegetable tray.

2	**pounds lean ground beef**
1	**medium onion, finely chopped**
4	**teaspoons chili powder**
1	**garlic clove, minced**
½	**teaspoon oregano, crushed fine**
2	**(16-oz) cans diced tomatoes, with liquid**

Brown ground beef and onions; drain. Stir in chili powder, garlic, oregano, and tomatoes. Simmer 2 to 3 hours. Makes 4 to 6 servings.

Stuffed Burgers

1½	pounds lean ground beef
1	cup (4-oz) Cheddar cheese, shredded
4	tablespoons barbecue sauce
4	hamburger buns

Divide meat into 8 equal portions and shape into thin patties.

Sprinkle cheese in center of half the patties. Press remaining patties over cheese and press to seal. Place on grill and cook to 160°F, turning once. Brush with barbecue sauce toward end of cooking time. Makes 4 servings.

Taco Burgers

1	pound lean ground beef
½	cup salsa
4	slices Cheddar cheese
4	hamburger buns
1	cup shredded lettuce
2	Plum tomatoes, chopped

Combine ground beef and salsa. Form ground beef into 4 patties, about ¾-inch thick. Broil or grill until cooked to 160°F. Top with cheese and place on buns.

Top each with lettuce and tomato. Makes 4 servings.

Grill

If desired, serve on a lettuce leaf with dill pickles.
Serve with potato salad, cole slaw or fresh fruit.

Broil or Grill

Safety First

Hamburgers, because they are made with ground meat must be cooked to an internal temperature of 160°F. This should kill any harmful bacteria. (Always use an accurate thermometer.) Cook any ground meat (beef, pork, poultry, etc.) to well done.

Southwestern Cheeseburgers

1½	pounds lean ground beef
¼	cup finely chopped onion
4	slices Pepper Jack cheese
4	tomato slices
4	hamburger buns

Combine ground beef and onion. Divide and shape into 8 thin slices. Top 4 patties with cheese, cutting cheese to fit. Cover with remaining patties and seal. Broil or grill until cooked to 160°F. Top with tomato slice and serve. Makes 4 servings.

Swiss-Dill Burgers

1	pound lean ground beef
2	tablespoons sour cream
¼	teaspoon dried dill weed
4	slices Swiss cheese
4	hamburger buns

Combine first 3 ingredients, mixing lightly. Shape into 4 patties and grill until cooked to 160°F. Top with cheese and cook until melted. Makes 4 servings.

"I don't like that!"

A complaint mothers often hear when the family sits down for dinner. You can eliminate some of this by preparing weekly menus and including your children in the choices. This not only provides them with something they like, but can help teach them meal planning and proper nutrition. You might even try the logic that you'll try their choices if they will try yours. Within reason, of course!

Sloppy Joes

2	pounds lean ground beef
1	cup finely chopped onion
¾	cup chili sauce
3	tablespoons prepared mustard
1	to 2 teaspoons chili powder, or to taste
	Hamburger buns

In a large skillet, cook ground beef and onion until browned; drain off fat. Add chili sauce, mustard, and chili powder, along with ½ *cup water*. Bring to a boil, reduce heat, and simmer 15 to 20 minutes or until liquid is absorbed, stirring occasionally. Serve on buns. Makes 6 to 8 sandwiches.

Stove Top

Prepare these for picnics, kid's birthday parties, and after game treats.

Reuben Burgers

1½	pounds lean ground beef
1	cup sauerkraut, drained
4	slices Swiss cheese
4	hamburger buns

Shape ground beef into 4 patties and grill or cook as desired, to 160°F.

Top each patty with sauerkraut, then cheese. Cover grill to melt the cheese.

Grill

To reduce calories; eliminate the bun. They are equally as good.

Crab Rolls

Cooked crab cut into bite-size pieces
Mayonnaise
Hot dog buns, toasted

Combine crab with enough mayonnaise to lightly coat. Fill buns with mixture and serve.

Variation:
Place mixture in pocket bread and add some chopped green onion and tomato slices.

Deli Sub Wrap

A meal in itself, but if really hungry, add dill pickles, raw vegetable sticks, and ½ cup fresh raspberries.

1	(7-inch) tortilla
2	slices deli roast beef
1	thin slice Jarlsberg cheese
½	cup alfalfa sprouts
1	teaspoon oil

Top each tortilla with the next 3 ingredients. Drizzle with oil (you may use less). Roll tightly.

Delicious Sandwich Combinations

Top focaccia bread with sliced chicken, bacon, Mozzarella, mushrooms and Italian dressing

Top French bread with sliced chicken, bacon, Swiss cheese, tomato, red onion and honey mustard dressing

Sliced turkey on sour dough with bacon, avocado slices, lettuce, tomato and Italian dressing

Top focaccia bread with grilled chicken, Provolone, toasted red peppers, fresh basil, lettuce and tomato

Roast beef in pocket bread with caramelized onions, watercress and ranch dressing

Tuna salad on marbled rye bread with Monterey Jack cheese and tomato.

Grilled steak slices on hoagie rolls topped with sautéed onions and peppers, white Cheddar cheese and BBQ or Sloppy Joe sauce

Special Turkey Sandwich

For each sandwich:

2	slices sourdough bread
1	tablespoon cream cheese, softened
2	tablespoons cranberry sauce
2	ounces deli sliced turkey
	Lettuce leaves

Spread one side of each bread slice with cream cheese. Spread with cranberry sauce. Add turkey and lettuce. Makes 1 sandwich.

Variation:
Substitute bagels for the sour-dough bread.

Turkey & Swiss Sandwich

2	tablespoons mayonnaise
8	slices pumpernickel or 7-grain bread
8	slices deli sliced turkey
8	slices bacon, cooked
4	slices Swiss cheese
4	to 8 thin slices tomato

Spread mayonnaise on bread slices. Layer with turkey, bacon, cheese, and tomato. Top with bread slice. Makes 4 sandwiches.

Make this sandwich special by using fresh grown tomatoes when in season.

Try using some of your own favorite ingredients and you might come up with some fantastic sandwich ideas.

Beef & Cheese Roll-ups

4	(7-inch) tortillas
½	cup soft herb cream cheese spread
8	slices deli roast beef
1	cup (4-oz) Monterey Jack cheese, shredded
2	cups shredded lettuce

Spread each tortilla with 2 tablespoons cheese spread. Top with ingredients in order listed. Roll tightly. Makes 4 servings

Juna-Egg Wraps

1	(12-oz) can white tuna, drained
¼	cup finely chopped onion
2	hardboiled eggs, chopped
⅓	cup mayonnaise (or to taste)
4	(7-inch) tortillas

Combine first 4 ingredients. Spread equal amounts on tortillas and roll tightly. Makes 4 servings

Dijonnaise

If you like both Dijon mustard and mayonnaise on your sandwiches, make your own Dijonnaise and keep on hand. All you have to do is mix ½ cup mayonnaise with 2 teaspoons Dijon mustard (or to taste).

Chicken-Alfalfa Wrap

1	(10-inch) tortilla
1	tablespoon mayonnaise
3	slices deli chicken
2	tablespoons Plum tomato, chopped
¼	cup alfalfa sprouts

Spread tortilla with 1 tablespoon mayonnaise. Layer with remaining ingredients. Roll tightly. Makes 1 wrap.

Soft Tacos

Stove Top

1	pound lean ground beef
4	(7-inch) tortillas
¾	cup (3-oz) Cheddar cheese, shredded
¼	cup sour cream
¼	cup salsa

Brown ground beef; drain. Spread beef in center of tortillas. Top with cheese, sour cream and salsa. Roll to enclose filling. Makes 4 servings

Serve immediately to prevent tortillas from getting too soft.

Sausage Wraps

Stove Top

1	(12-oz) package sausage
⅓	cup chopped onions
1	(4-oz) can sliced mushrooms, drained, chopped
4	(7-inch) tortillas
1	cup (4-oz) Monterey Jack cheese, shredded

Brown sausage and onion; drain. Add mushrooms and heat through. Place ¼ of mixture on each tortilla; sprinkle with cheese. Roll tightly. Makes 4 servings.

Variation:
Substitute ground beef for the sausage.

Guacamole Spread

This makes a nice spread for wraps.

1	ripe avocado, mashed
1	tablespoon thick and chunky salsa

Combine ingredients and use as a spread on tortillas or sandwiches.

Taco Burger Wraps

1	pound lean ground beef
½	cup thick and chunky salsa
4	(7-inch) tortillas
¾	cup (3-oz) Cheddar cheese, shredded
3	Plum tomatoes, chopped
1	cup shredded lettuce

Brown ground beef; drain. Add salsa and simmer until liquid is absorbed. Fill with meat mixture and layer with cheese, tomatoes, and lettuce. Roll tightly. Makes 4 servings.

Bread Bowl Sandwich

Are you tired of doing the same old thing for picnics? Give this a try…it's a little different and great for those hungry appetites.

Note: You can vary the type and size of the bread loaf, as well as the filling.

Sandwich for two:

1	(5 to 6-inch) round loaf sour dough bread, unsliced
1	tablespoon mayonnaise
4	ounces deli sliced turkey
1	small Plum tomato, sliced
	Lettuce

Cut a 1 to 1½-inch slice from top of bread. Remove bread from center, leaving a ¼-inch shell. Spread inside of shell with mayonnaise. Arrange folded slices of turkey on bottom. Top with tomato slices, then lettuce. Replace top. Cut in half to serve. Makes 2 servings.

Hot Dog Wrap

Makes 1 serving

1	hot dog
1	(1-oz) slice Cheddar cheese, halved
1	to 2 teaspoons prepared mustard
1	tablespoon dill pickle relish
1	(7-inch) tortilla

Split hot dog lengthwise. Place, cut-side down, in small skillet and brown, turning once. Top with cheese and let melt.

Spread tortilla with mustard. Place hot dog in center and top with relish. Roll tightly.

Turkey Club Wrap

A restaurant favorite.

1	(7-inch) tortilla
1	tablespoon mayonnaise
2	slices deli turkey
2	slices bacon, cooked, crumbled
1	Plum tomato, chopped
½	cup shredded lettuce

Spread tortilla with mayonnaise. Layer ingredients in order listed. Roll tightly. Makes 1 wrap.

Stove Top

These are surprisingly good using the oh-so-popular tortilla instead of the hot dog bun.

Hot Dogs

For variety, top hot dogs with the following ingredients:

- Chili, Cheddar cheese, diced onions

- Sautéed onions

- Sauerkraut and caraway seeds

- Mustard, relish, chopped onion, peppers, and pickle spears (Chicago style)

- Sauerkraut and Swiss cheese

Broil

Tip: When cutting sandwiches, use a sharp or serrated knife to avoid squashing the bread.

English Muffin Treats

2	English muffins, split and toasted
	Mayonnaise
4	(¼-inch) tomato slices
4	thin onion slices
4	slices of Cheddar cheese
4	slices of bacon, cooked and broken in half

Spread muffins with mayonnaise. Layer with slices of tomato, onion, and cheese. Place under broiler to melt cheese. Top each with 2 strips of bacon and serve. Makes 4 sandwiches.

Broil

These delightful muffins are surprisingly delicious. They do take a little more time to prepare, but are worth it.

Banana–Muffin Treat

4	English muffins
	Butter
2	bananas, sliced
8	slices Swiss cheese
8	slices bacon, cooked, broken in half

Toast, then lightly butter the muffins and place on a baking sheet. Arrange banana slices on muffins. Top with a slice of cheese. Criss-cross 2 slices bacon on top of cheese. Place under broiler just long enough to melt the cheese. Makes 2 to 4 servings.

Make Ahead Toasted Cheese Sandwiches

Sliced cheese
Sliced bread
Melted butter

Do ahead: Place cheese between bread slices. Place on a baking pan and cover tightly. Chill until ready to serve.

When ready to serve, brush both sides lightly with butter. Place under broiler and broil each side until just golden.

Tip: I have tried baking the sandwiches, but I think broiling is better for a crispy golden brown sandwich.

This is the easiest way I know, to make a lot of sandwiches quickly.

New Hot Turkey Sandwich

1	cup whipping cream
1½	cups (6-oz) Brie cheese
	Salt and pepper
	Turkey slices, heated, enough for 4 sandwiches
4	(1-inch) slices French bread, lightly toasted, if desired
1	cup fresh spinach leaves

Heat whipping cream in medium saucepan; bring to a boil. Remove from heat.

While cream is heating, remove rind from Brie and cut cheese into small cubes. Gradually add to the cream, stirring to melt. Season with salt and pepper.

Place bread slices on serving plates. Top with spinach, then the turkey slices. Spoon sauce over top. Makes 4 servings.

Stove Top

Different, but oh so good! Great for Thanksgiving leftovers. Serve with cranberry sauce, stuffing and pumpkin pie.

Grilled Reuben Sandwiches

12	to 16 slices deli corned beef
8	slices dark rye bread
1	(8-oz) can sauerkraut, well drained
½	cup Thousand Island dressing
4	slices Swiss cheese
	Melted butter

Arrange 3 to 4 slices corned beef on 4 slices of the bread. Top each with ¼ of the sauerkraut. Drizzle with ¼ of the dressing and top with cheese. Top with remaining bread slices.

Brush both sides of bread with melted butter. Place in a heated nonstick skillet and lightly brown both sides. Check the cheese, but at this point it should be melted. Makes 4 sandwiches.

Chicken Club Sandwich

4	chicken breast halves, skinned, boned
3	tablespoons olive oil, divided
4	slices Swiss cheese
4	sandwich rolls, split
8	thin tomato slices
8	slices cooked bacon

Flatten chicken breasts to an even thickness. Cook in 2 tablespoons of the oil until cooked through, turning once. Place cheese on top and remove chicken from skillet.

Drizzle cut side of rolls with remaining oil. Top bottom halves with 2 slices of tomato, chicken and then bacon. Makes 4 servings.

Polish Sausage Hoagies

1	tablespoon olive oil
¾	cup chopped onion
¼	cup chopped green pepper
⅓	cup drained sauerkraut
2	cooked Polish sausages, heated
2	hot dog buns or hard rolls

Heat oil in small skillet. Cook onion and green pepper until just tender. Add sauerkraut and heat through. Place sausages on buns and top with vegetable mixture. Makes 2 servings.

Stove Top

Serve with coleslaw, fresh vegetable sticks and your favorite pickles.

Chicken Pesto Pizza

1	(13.8-oz) refrigerated pizza crust
⅓	cup pesto
1½	cups (6-oz) Mozzarella cheese, shredded
1½	cups cubed cooked chicken
1	(6-oz) jar marinated artichokes, drained.
3	Plum tomatoes, chopped

Place pizza crust on baking sheet and spread with pesto. Sprinkle with remaining ingredients in order given and bake 10 to 15 minutes or until crust is golden brown and cheese is melted. Makes 4 to 6 servings.

Oven 425°F

Variation: Substitute barbecue sauce for the pesto and chopped green pepper for the arti-chokes.

Boredom Buster

To prevent boredom and to help kids be not-so-picky, try to prepare 1 to 2 new recipes a week. This could be a main dish or a side dish. Perhaps even a simple dessert. (It's not as difficult as it sounds - you just need to plan ahead.)

Stove Top
Oven 450°F

These are best served in small servings with soup or salad or as an appetizer.

Deep Dish Pizza

3	cups baking mix
¾	cup cold water
1½	pounds lean ground beef
½	cup finely chopped onion
1	(14-oz) jar pizza sauce or spaghetti sauce
1	(12-oz) package Mozzarella cheese, shredded

Mix baking mix and water until soft dough form; beat 20 strokes. Place on floured board and knead about 20 times. With floured hands, press dough evenly on bottom and up sides of a sprayed 15x10-inch jelly roll pan.

Lightly brown ground beef and onions; drain off fat. Spread pizza sauce over dough. Distribute meat over top. Sprinkle with cheese. Bake about 20 minutes or until lightly browned. Watch cheese carefully the last 5 minutes. Makes 6 to 8 servings.

Garlic Bread Pizza Wedge

1	(14-oz) purchased, Italian pizza crust
⅓	cup finely chopped red onion
2	large garlic cloves, minced
1	teaspoon dried oregano, crushed
1	cup mayonnaise
1	cup freshly grated Parmesan cheese

Place bread shell on an ungreased 14-inch pizza pan.

Cook onion in a small amount of water until softened.

Combine onion with remaining ingredients and spread over the crust. Bake 8 to 10 minutes or until quite golden and the bottom of the shell has become crisp. Cut into 24 wedges. Serve hot. Makes 24 servings.

Beef, Pork & Seafood

Menu Ideas

Organization is the key to stress-free cooking. In the long run, it will save you time as well as money.

Make it simple and plan a 4-week cycle of menus. Once this is done, the hardest part is over and you are on your way to preparing more nutritious meals for your family.

As long as you know what the main course is, filling in the rest is fairly easy. At least once a week, prepare a ham, roast, chicken or turkey and plan for the use of leftovers.

A sample weekly menu might be:

Sunday	Ham
Monday	Pizza
Tuesday	Ham & Noodle Casserole*
Wednesday	Roasted Chicken*
Thursday	Crab Divan*
Friday	Au Gratin New Potato Casserole* (add leftover ham)
Saturday	Italian Chicken Casserole*

You can also assemble this recipe in two 8x8-inch square pans and freeze one. Half of the recipe will make 6 servings.

Company Beef Casserole

1½	pounds lean ground beef
1	(15½-oz) jar spaghetti sauce
12	ounces small egg noodles
1	(3-oz) package cream cheese, softened
1	cup sour cream
16	ounces Mozzarella cheese, shredded

Brown ground beef; drain. Add spaghetti sauce; simmer 20 minutes.

Meanwhile, cook noodles; drain

Beat cream cheese until smooth. Add sour cream; mix well. Spread half the noodles in sprayed 13x9-inch baking dish. Cover with half the cream cheese mixture; top with half the cheese. Spread all the meat sauce over cheese. Layer remaining noodles, cream cheese mixture and cheese. Bake 30 minutes or until heated through. Makes 12 servings.

For a colorful, festive dish, use red, yellow and orange peppers.

Note: Any leftover meat mixture can be spooned around the peppers.

Stuffed Green Peppers

1½	pounds lean ground beef
1	cup chopped onion
½	cup cooked rice
	Salt and pepper to taste
4	large green peppers
2	(8-oz) cans tomato sauce

In a skillet, brown ground beef and onion; drain. Add cooked rice and season to taste.

Meanwhile, cut green peppers in half lengthwise. Remove seeds. Place cut-side up, in sprayed 13x9-inch baking dish. Fill with meat mixture. Pour tomato sauce over top. *Add ¼ cup water* to baking dish. Bake 60 minutes or until peppers are tender. Makes 8 servings.

Everyone's Favorite Lasagne

Stove Top
Oven 375°F

2	pounds lean ground beef
1	tablespoon brown sugar
1	(28-oz) jar chunky spaghetti sauce with mushrooms, about 3 cups
8	lasagne noodles, cooked
2½	cups (10-oz) Cheddar Cheese, shredded
3	cups (12-oz) Mozzarella cheese, shredded

Brown ground beef in a large skillet; drain off fat. Stir in brown sugar and spaghetti sauce. Bring to a boil; reduce heat and simmer 20 minutes.

In a sprayed 13x9-inch baking dish, spread about ½ cup of the meat sauce. Layer, starting with half the noodles, sauce and cheeses, making 2 layers of everything.

Cover with foil. Bake 30 minutes; remove foil, bake 10 to 15 minutes or until hot and bubbly. Makes 10 to 12 servings.

An excellent lasagne dish that doesn't take all day to make. You can use the "Oven Ready" lasagne noodles, just be sure to read the box as some brands may require additional water and or sauce.

Make 2 - Freeze 1

For quick emergency meals, always have a lasagne or other precooked meal in the freezer. For individual servings: bake lasagne, cool, slice into desired size squares and wrap tightly in plastic wrap. Remove amount needed, thaw and reheat.

If desired, cook on an outdoor grill and serve with a mushroom sauce. For mock Filet Mignon, wrap 1 slice of bacon around each patty before cooking. Serve with baked potatoes and tossed green salad.

Stove Top

This recipe will be a standby for many busy cooks. It makes a lot, which also makes for wonderful leftovers. To make ahead: Prepare as directed and spoon into a sprayed 13x9-inch baking dish. When ready to serve, bake at 350°F for 30 minutes. Add cheese and bake about 5 minutes.

Salisbury Steak

1½	pounds lean ground beef
¾	cup quick cooking oats
¼	cup finely chopped onions
1	large egg, beaten
½	cup tomato juice
	Salt and pepper to taste

Combine ingredients in large mixing bowl. Shape into 4 thick oval patties. Place on broiler rack and cook to 160°F, turning once. Makes 4 servings.

Ground Beef Salsa Dinner

8	ounces rotini noodles
1½	pounds lean ground beef
1	cup chopped onion
2	cups salsa
1	(11-oz) can Mexicorn, drained
1	cup (4-oz) Cheddar cheese, shredded

Cook pasta according to package directions; drain.

Meanwhile, in a 12-inch deep skillet, brown ground beef and onion; drain. Add salsa and corn; heat through. Add pasta, then sprinkle with cheese. Cover and cook 5 minutes or until cheese is melted. Makes 6 to 8 large servings.

Beefy Pasta Bake

Stove Top
Oven 350°F

1½	pounds lean ground beef
¾	cup finely chopped onion
1	cup sour cream
1	(10¾-oz) can Cream of Mushroom soup
1	(10¾-oz) can Cream of Chicken soup
5	cups rotini noodles, cooked, drained

Brown ground beef and onion in large skillet; drain off fat. Stir in remaining ingredients.

Pour into a sprayed 3-quart casserole or 13x9-inch baking dish. Bake 45 minutes or until heated through. Makes 6 to 8 servings.

Note: If really in a hurry, heat ingredients in skillet and omit step two.

You can do all kinds of things with this casserole. Add any combination of chopped green pepper, pimiento, olives, corn, peas, etc. Use regular or spiral shaped noodles, top with buttered soft bread crumbs or grated cheese. Or, just follow the recipe.

Ever Changing Ingredients

It seems food manufactures are constantly changing their products. The most common change recently has been Down Sizing. A standard jar of spaghetti sauce used to be 32 ounces. It was then reduced to 30 then 28 and, as of this book, many are 26 ounces. This Down Sizing can play havoc with your recipes, especially those from older cookbooks when ingredients were packaged in larger quantities.

Skillet Lasagne

10	ounces mafalda pasta
1	pound lean ground beef
1	(15.5-oz) jar chunky spaghetti sauce
1	tablespoon firmly packed brown sugar
1	cup (4-oz) Mozzarella cheese, shredded

A quick version of a family favorite. Serve with a salad and toasted French bread and you have a meal in minutes.

Note: Mafalda pasta looks like tiny lasagne noodles about 1-inch long.

Cook pasta according to package directions; drain.

Meanwhile, cook ground beef in a deep 10 or 12" skillet; drain off fat. Stir in spaghetti sauce and brown sugar. Bring to a boil, reduce heat and simmer 10 to 15 minutes. Add pasta to the sauce. You may or may not need all of the pasta. Stir to mix well and heat through. Sprinkle with cheese. Cover and heat long enough to melt the cheese. Makes 6 to 8 servings.

Southwestern Beef & Rice

1	pound lean ground beef
1	cup cooked rice
1	(15-oz) can kidney beans, drained
1	cup thick and chunky salsa
½	cup (2-oz) Cheddar cheese, shredded

Can be made in about 15 minutes and is a lot better than Hamburger Helper.

In a large skillet, brown ground beef; drain off fat. Add rice, kidney beans, and salsa; heat through. Add cheese and stir just until melted. Makes 6 servings.

Quick Meat Loaf

Oven 350°F

1½	pounds lean ground beef
1½	teaspoons salt
¼	teaspoon pepper
½	cup quick-cooking oats
¼	cup milk
1	large egg, lightly beaten

Serve with mashed potatoes, green beans, and a molded fruit salad.

Combine ingredients and shape into a loaf in a sprayed 13x9-inch baking dish. Bake 45 to 60 minutes or until meat reaches 160°F. Makes 6 servings.

Chili–Cornbread Casserole

Stove Top
Oven 400°F

2	(15-oz) cans chili with beans
1	(11-oz) can Mexicorn, drained
1	box (8½-oz) corn muffin mix
1	large egg
⅓	cup milk

Another pantry type recipe - choose your favorite brand of chili and if the Mexicorn is too hot for you, use 1 cup frozen or canned corn, drained.

Heat chili and corn in medium saucepan. Pour into a sprayed 11x7-inch baking dish. Combine corn muffin mix with egg and milk; combine just until moistened. Spread evenly as possible over the chili. Bake 12 to 15 minutes or until golden. Makes 4 to 6 servings.

Use those Leftovers

Leftover meat loaf can be used for not only sandwiches, but can be crumbled and used in spaghetti, chili, soup, pizza toppings, etc.

Skillet Ground Beef & Potatoes

1	pound lean ground beef
½	cup chopped onion
3	cups frozen O'Brien potatoes, thawed
1¼	cups salsa

In a large skillet, brown ground beef and onion; drain. Add potatoes and cook 8 to 10 minutes or until tender. Add salsa and heat through. Makes 4 large servings.

Beefy Italian Pasta

1½	pounds lean ground beef
1	(14.5-oz) can diced Italian tomatoes, with juice
1	teaspoon salt
¼	teaspoon pepper
2	cups uncooked rotini
12	ounces process cheese spread, cubed (optional)

In a large skillet (with a lid), brown ground beef; drain.

Add tomatoes, salt and pepper and bring to a boil. Add pasta and reduce heat to a medium simmer. Cover and cook 12 to 15 minutes or until pasta is tender and most of the liquid is absorbed.

If using, stir in the cheese and heat through until melted. Makes 6 servings.

If using the cheese, you may want to omit the salt.

Ground Beef Stove Top Dinner

1   (7.2-oz) box rice pilaf or beef flavored
        rice mix
1   pound lean ground beef
½   cup chopped celery
¾   cup chopped onion
½   cup (2-oz) Cheddar or Monterey Jack cheese,
        shredded

Cook rice according to directions on package. Meanwhile, brown ground beef, celery, and onion in a deep 10-inch skillet; drain off fat. Add rice, and if necessary, cook a little longer to heat through. Sprinkle cheese over top. Cover and let stand until cheese has melted. Makes 6 servings.

Stove Top

Nothing fancy here, but you'll enjoy this quick and easy recipe on those days when you have to eat and run.

Dinner Nachos

¾   pound lean ground beef
⅓   cup taco sauce
4   cups tortilla chips
1   small tomato, coarsely chopped
⅓   cup sliced ripe olives
2   cups (8-oz) Cheddar cheese, shredded

Lightly brown ground beef; drain. Add taco sauce.

Spread tortilla chips on a 12-inch pizza pan or large baking sheet. Spoon meat over top. Sprinkle with tomato, olives, and then cheese. Bake 10 minutes or until cheese is melted. Serves 2 for dinner; 4 for snacks.

Stove Top
Oven 400°F

The all-in-one meal doesn't really need anything except perhaps a light dessert.

This is a very old recipe, but when my granddaughter, Paulina, had it for the first time at a friend's house, she loved it. I decided to bring it out of my file box for everyone to enjoy.

Tater Tot Casserole

1½	pounds lean ground beef
1	medium onion, thinly sliced
	Salt and pepper
1	can Cream of Celery or Mushroom soup
1	(16-oz) package Tater Tots

In a skillet, brown the ground beef, then drain. Spoon into a sprayed 11x7-inch baking dish.

Separate onion slices into rings and arrange over meat. Sprinkle with salt and pepper. Give the soup a stir and spread over onion. Cover with Tater Tots. Bake 30 to 40 minutes or until heated through. Makes 6 servings.

Really Quick Meals

Taco Salad
Purchased Roasted Chicken
Hamburgers, salad, fresh veggies
Quick Homemade Soup
Easy Skillet Dinner
Purchased Fried Chicken - add coleslaw and baked beans
Chicken, Beef or Pork kabobs

Have on Hand in Freezer

Breaded chicken strips and nuggets
Marinated chicken breast or flank steak
Homemade soups
Casseroles
Spaghetti sauce
Cooked chicken cubes or strips
(use in Caesar salad, fajitas, casseroles, etc.)

Cooking Beef

The best guarantee, for the best results, when cooking any meat is an accurate thermometer. Time charts are good guidelines, but there can be several variables:

- How cold is the meat? (Was it just removed from the refrigerator or has it been sitting out at room temperature)
- Is your oven temperature accurate?
- Is the cut long and narrow or short and thick?

A thermometer is the best way to ensure the same degree of doneness time after time. Experiment to find just the right temperature that your family prefers.

REMOVE AT:

"I have found that removing the meat from the source of heat when it reaches 135°F, covering it with foil and allowing it to stand 10 to 15 minutes produces MEDIUM RARE and removing it at 140°F produces MEDIUM."

For juiciest meat always allow the 10 to 15 minutes standing time.

The temperature will rise during standing time.

Cut of Meat	Weight (pounds)	Oven Temp.	Approx. Cooking Time Medium rare (135°F)	Medium (140°)
Eye Round Roast	2-3	325°F	1½-1¾ hrs	not advised
Rib Eye Roast (small end)	4-6 6-8	350°F	1¾-2 hrs 2-2½ hrs	2-2½ hrs 2½-3 hrs
Rib Eye Roast (large end)	4-6 6-8	350°F	2-2½ hrs 2¼-2½ hrs	2½-3 hrs 2¾-3¼ hrs
Rib Roast (Prime rib)	6-8 8-10	350°F	2¼-2½ hrs 2½-3 hrs	2¾-3 hrs 3-3½ hrs
Round Tip Roast	4-6 6-8	325°F	2-2½ hrs 2½-3 hrs	2½-3 hrs 3-3½ hrs
Tenderloin	2-3 4-5	425°F	35-40 min. 50-60 min.	45-50 min. 60-70 min.
Tri-Tip Roast	1½-2	425°F	30-40 min.	40-45 min.

Basic Pot Roast

Stove Top
Oven 350°F

We all need a good
basic pot roast
recipe.

1	(3 to 4-lb) rump roast
¼	cup oil
1	medium onion, sliced
	Salt and pepper to taste
1½	teaspoons mixed herbs

Brown in heated oil in a heavy pot or dutch oven. Add remaining ingredients along with *1 cup water*. Cover and bake 2 to 2½ hours or until meat is tender, adding more water if necessary.

Pepper Roast

Oven 350°F

A sirloin roast is best
when thinly sliced.
And even better
when served with
mashed potatoes,
gravy and green
beans.

2	pound sirloin tip roast
2½	teaspoons seasoned salt
3	teaspoons coarsely ground black pepper

Rub meat with salt and pepper. Place on a rack in a small roasting pan. Bake about 60 minutes or until temperature reaches 135°F for medium rare and 140°F for medium. Cover with foil and let stand 10 to 15 minutes for easier carving.

Standing Rib Roast

Oven 350°F

Always an elegant
meal. Serve with
scalloped potatoes,
broccoli, your favorite
salad and rolls.

1	standing prime rib roast (4 ribs)
	Seasoning, if desired

Place roast, rib-side down, on rack in a shallow roasting pan. Sprinkle with seasoning, if using. Bake to 135°F for medium rare and 140°F for medium. Cover lightly with foil and let stand 15 to 20 minutes before slicing.

Rump Roast

Oven 325ºF

1   (4-lb) boneless rump roast
     Salt and pepper

Place roast, fat-side up, on rack in a shallow roasting pan. Sprinkle with salt and pepper. Bake 2 to 2½ hours or until temperature reaches 135°F for medium rare or 140°F for medium. Let stand 10 minutes before slicing. Makes 8 servings.

Tip: To make Au Jus, skim off excess fat from meat juices. Add a little water to pan. Bring to a simmer and cook 3 to 4 minutes, stirring in the crusty pieces. Strain.

A rump roast is often called something else, depending on where you live.

Grilled Flank Steak

1   (1 to 1¼-lb) flank steak
1   tablespoon oil
2   tablespoons honey
2   tablespoons soy sauce
1   orange (¼ cup juice and 1 teaspoon grated zest)
¼   teaspoon ground ginger

Trim flank steak of any fat or silver skin. Place in a large resealable plastic bag.

Combine remaining ingredients and pour into bag. Seal and place in a baking dish (to catch any leaks). Marinate 4 to 6 hours, occasionally turning the bag.

Remove meat from marinade (discard marinade) and cook on hot grill about 4 to 6 minutes per side or to desired doneness, bearing in mind that if flank steak is cooked much past medium rare it may be tough. Thinly slice across the grain. Makes 4 servings.

**Marinate
Grill**

Why not prepare a second flank steak for the freezer. Simply put steak and marinade in freezer bag and place in freezer. Then, on a busy day, simply thaw and grill.

Marinate
Broil or Grill

Serve with baked
potatoes and fresh
green beans.

Teriyaki Flank Steak

1	(1 to 1½-lb) flank steak
1	cup firmly packed brown sugar
1	cup soy sauce
5	slices fresh ginger
1	garlic clove, minced
½	cup pineapple juice

Combine ingredients in shallow dish. Cover and marinate at least 2 hours or overnight in refrigerator. Discard marinade.

Broil or grill to desired degree of doneness. Makes 4 servings.

Stove Top
Oven 350°F

Let bake in the oven
while you are busy
doing other things.
Serve with rice or
noodles, peas and
a tossed salad or a
gelatin salad.

Swiss Steak

1	(2-lb) round steak, 1-inch thick
	Salt and pepper
3	tablespoons oil
½	cup chopped onion
1	(16-oz) can diced tomatoes, with juice

Sprinkle meat with salt and pepper.

Heat oil in a Dutch oven or large skillet; add meat and brown both sides. Top with onion and tomatoes. Cover and bake 1½ to 2 hours or until tender, adding water if necessary. Makes 6 servings

Teriyaki Tri-Tip Steaks

Marinate
Broil or Grill

Allow time for meat to marinate 6 to 8 hours.

1½	pounds tri-tip beef steak
½	cup soy sauce
2	tablespoons brown sugar
½	teaspoon ground ginger

Place meat in a large resealable bag. Combine remaining ingredients with ¼ *cup water*. Pour over meat. Seal. Marinate in refrigerator for 6 to 8 hours. Discard marinade.

Grill over hot coals until cooked to desired doneness, turning once. Makes 4 servings.

Beef Stroganoff

Stove Top

If the beef broth isn't a full flavored broth, you may want to season with a little salt and pepper.

1½	pounds beef tenderloin or top sirloin
6	tablespoons butter, divided
1	cup chopped onion
¼	cup flour
1¾	cups beef broth
1	cup sour cream

Cut meat across the grain into ¼-inch strips about 1½-inches long.

Heat butter in large skillet. Add onion and cook until tender; remove and set aside. Add remaining butter to skillet. Add half the meat and lightly brown; remove and repeat with remaining meat. Return all the meat to skillet, but do not drain off fat.

Add onion and flour to skillet; stir to mix. Slowly add the broth, stirring until smooth. Cook until thickened, stirring occasionally. Reduce heat. Add sour cream and heat through, but do not boil or it may curdle. Serve over rice or noodles. Makes 4 to 6 servings.

Beef Kabobs

1	(1½-lb) top sirloin
1	cup dry white wine
⅔	cup olive oil
⅓	cup soy sauce
2	large garlic cloves, minced
1	medium onion (8 wedges)

If using wooden skewers, don't forget to soak in water for about 20 minutes.

Cut meat into 16 (1½-inch) cubes. Combine next 4 ingredients. Reserve ¼ cup for basting. Add meat; cover and marinate in refrigerator at least 2 hours. Discard marinade.

Thread the meat and onion on 4 skewers. Place on grill or under broiler and cook to desired doneness or about 3 minutes per side, basting frequently with the ¼ cup sauce. Makes 4 servings.

Marinate
Broil, Grill or
Stove Top

Beef Fajitas

1	pound skirt steak, flank steak, or top sirloin
½	cup fresh lime juice
¾	teaspoon garlic salt
½	teaspoon freshly ground black pepper
	Flour tortillas, warmed

This is a popular recipe in restaurants, as well as home entertaining. Chicken breast halves can be substituted for the beef. Favorite condiments served with Fajitas are: guacamole, salsa, chopped onion, and tomato or sour cream. Also, grilled onions and peppers.

Place beef in shallow dish. Combine next 3 ingredients and pour over meat. Cover and refrigerate several hours or overnight.

Remove meat from marinade; drain thoroughly. Cook to desired degree of doneness. Meat can be grilled, broiled, or cooked in a skillet with a small amount of oil. Slice diagonally into thin strips. Serve with warm flour tortillas. Makes 4 servings.

Cooking Pork

The fear of trichinosis was, at one time, associated with eating under cooked pork. Today, the safety of pork has greatly improved. The trichinosis organism is destroyed at an internal temperature of 137°F which is well below the recommended cooked temperature of 150°F to 165°F. Keep in mind that meat will continue to cook and the temperature will continue to rise after removing from the oven.

REMOVE AT:

"I have found that removing the pork from the source of heat when it reaches 145°F, covering it loosely with foil and allowing it to stand 10 to 15 minutes produces the best results."

For juiciest meat always allow the 10 to 15 minutes standing time.

The temperature will rise during standing time.

Cut	Oven Temperature	Pounds	Remove at:	Approx. cooking time (minutes per pound)
Crown Roast	350°F	6-10	145°F	18-22
Center Loin Roast	350°F	3-5	145°F	18-22
Boneless Top Loin Roast	350°F	2-4	145°F	18-22
Whole Leg (Fresh ham)	350°F	12	180°F	18-22
Tenderloin	425°F	½-1½	145°F	25-35 minutes Total cooking time
Half Ham (Fully cooked)	325°F	6-8	140°F	60 minutes Total cooking time

Pork Roast Dijon

1	(2½-lb) boneless pork loin roast
2	teaspoons Dijon mustard
½	teaspoon dried rosemary
	Salt and pepper

Place roast on a rack in a roasting pan; spread with mustard and sprinkle with rosemary, salt, and pepper.

Bake 40 to 50 minutes or until meat reaches 145°F. Cover loosely with foil and let stand 15 minutes before slicing. Makes 6 servings.

Roasted Pork Shoulder

7	pound picnic shoulder
	Salt and pepper

Trim pork of excess fat. Sprinkle with salt and pepper. Place on a rack in a roasting pan.

Bake about 4 hours or to 185°F, brushing occasionally with drippings. Cover loosely with foil; let stand 20 minutes before slicing. Makes 8 to 10 servings.

Grilled Pineapple

Grill fresh pineapple slices, brushing frequently with melted butter, turning once. Maybe even try basting with equal amounts of butter and brown sugar.

Italian Sausage Dinner

Stove Top

4	Italian sausages
1	tablespoon oil
1	small onion, sliced
1	small green pepper, sliced
4	Plum tomatoes, sliced
	Salt and pepper

Brown sausages in hot oil in a medium skillet. Add onion and green pepper and cook until vegetables are just crisp-tender. Add tomatoes, salt, and pepper and heat through. Makes 4 servings.

Hearty and flavorful.

Variation:
Serve in Hoagie rolls or toasted French bread.

Cashew Ham Bake

Oven 300°F

1	large ham slice, 1-inch thick
½	cup orange marmalade
¼	cup coarsely chopped cashews

Place ham in a sprayed roasting pan. Bake 30 minutes.

Spread marmalade over the top and sprinkle with cashews. Bake 15 minutes. Makes 4 to 6 servings.

Note: Serve with buttered peas, Dinner Hash Browns, and a crisp green salad.

Hot Dogs & Sauerkraut

Oven 350°F

1	(32-oz) jar sauerkraut, drained
2	teaspoons caraway seeds
8	hot dogs
1½	cups (6-oz) Swiss cheese, shredded

Place sauerkraut in a sprayed 11x7-inch baking dish. Sprinkle with caraway seeds and mix with a fork. Arrange hot dogs over top and sprinkle with cheese. Bake 25 to 35 minutes or until heated through. Makes 4 servings.

The caraway seeds and Swiss cheese softens the tartness of the sauerkraut.

Delicious Baby Back Ribs

1   **rack of baby back ribs**
     Salt and pepper

Trim ribs and pat dry. Sprinkle both sides rather generously with the salt and pepper.

Place in a shallow roasting pan, meaty-side down, in a single layer. Bake 30 minutes. Turn ribs and bake 30 to 40 minutes or until very tender. The cooking time may vary according to the number of ribs in the pan and how hot your oven cooks. For easier slicing, wrap in foil and let stand 15 to 20 minutes. Makes 2 to 3 servings.

Maple Ham

1   **(7-lb) fully cooked bone-in ham**
1   **teaspoon dry mustard**
2   **teaspoons cider vinegar**
½   **cup maple syrup**

Trim ham of excess fat. Score top of ham. Place, fat-side up, on a rack in a shallow roasting pan.

Bake 15 to 20 minutes per pound or until temperature reaches 140°F, about 1½ hours.

Meanwhile, combine remaining ingredients and spoon over ham last 30 minutes of cooking time. I usually add this after ham has baked about an hour. Then I baste a couple of times. Let stand 10 minutes before slicing. Makes about 10 servings.

Ham–Noodle Casserole

Stove Top
Oven 350°F

A quick economical meal.

8	ounces penne
½	cup sliced green onions
2	large eggs, lightly beaten
1	cup sour cream
¾	cup (3-oz) Swiss cheese, shredded
1½	cups cubed ham

Cook pasta according to package directions. Rinse and drain.

Cook onion in a small sprayed skillet until just tender.

Combine eggs and sour cream. Add onion, cheese and ham. Add pasta and mix well. Pour into a sprayed 2-quart casserole. Cover and bake 30 minutes. Uncover and bake 10 to 15 minutes or until heated through. Makes 8 servings.

Franks & Cornbread

Oven 400°F
Stove Top

Convenience foods are here to stay. Enjoy them for what they are, especially on those busy days when time is short.

1	large egg
⅓	cup milk
1	(8½-oz) box corn muffin mix
4	hot dogs
½	cup (2-oz) Cheddar cheese, shredded
1	(16-oz) can chili with beans (optional)

Combine first 3 ingredients, mixing just until moistened. Spoon into a sprayed 8x8-inch baking dish.

Cut hot dogs in half lengthwise, but do not cut all the way through. Open flat and place on top of batter, cutting, if necessary, to fit dish. Sprinkle with cheese. Bake 15 to 20 minutes or until golden.

Meanwhile, heat chili. Cut cornbread into squares. Top each serving with some of the chili. Makes 4 servings.

Chicken Fried Pork

2   **thick cut (1-1½-inches) boneless pork chops**
      Salt and pepper
½   **cup flour**
      Vegetable oil

This recipe can be made for any number of servings, using any size boneless pork, pounded to ¼-inch thick.

Note: For a traditional Southern dinner, serve with mashed potatoes, green beans, biscuits and how about Deep Dish Fruit Cobbler.

Cut pork into 2 thin chops. Place between plastic wrap and pound to ¼-inch thickness. Sprinkle both sides with salt and pepper. Dredge in flour, coating both sides and shaking off excess.

Heat ¼-inch oil in a heavy large skillet. Add pork and cook until nicely browned, about 3 to 4 minutes on each side. Makes 4 servings.

Note: If gravy is desired, pour off all but 2 tablespoons of the fat. Add 1 cup milk. Heat until boiling, scraping up all the browned bits. Cook until thickened. (No need to add flour, as the flour from the cooked pork chops is usually enough to thicken the gravy.)

Menu
✳ ✳ ✳

Baked Salmon Steaks

Applesauce

Garlic Mashed Potatoes

Lemon Broccoli

Rice Chex Dessert

Cooking Time for Fish

Measure fish at its thickest point
Estimate 10 minutes total cooking time per inch at 450ºF

If baking a salmon or other fish and the fish measures 3 inches at its thickest point, bake 30 minutes at 450ºF. If broiling a steak 1½-inches thick, divide the total time in half and broil 7½ minutes on each side. Cooking time may vary somewhat according to the thickness and size of the fish, the temperature of the fish at cooking time and how accurate your oven temperature is. Watch carefully, and remember that fish will continue to cook somewhat after removing from heat. The internal temperature of fish should reach 137ºF.

Baked Salmon Steaks

Oven 450°F

4	**(6-oz) salmon steaks**
2	**tablespoons butter, melted**
½	**teaspoon Worcestershire sauce**
1	**teaspoon fresh lemon juice**

Salmon is one of the "good for you" high fat fish.

Place salmon in a sprayed shallow baking pan.

Combine remaining ingredients and brush salmon with some of the sauce. Bake 10 minutes, basting occasionally with the sauce. Test for doneness after 8 minutes. Makes 4 servings.

Pesto Salmon

Oven 450°F

6	**tablespoons pesto**
2	**(6-oz) salmon fillets, skinned**

Husband's night to cook.

Spread 3 tablespoons pesto in a sprayed 8x8-inch baking dish. Add salmon and spread with remaining pesto. Bake 10 to 12 minutes or until cooked through. Makes 2 servings.

A great Pacific Northwest treat.

Tip: Salmon cooked in foil or stuffed may take a little longer to cook.

Note: The number of servings will depend on the size of the fish.

Baked Whole Salmon

Whole salmon, cleaned, wiped dry
Salt & pepper
1   large lemon, sliced
1   medium onion, sliced
6   slices bacon

Sprinkle salmon with salt and pepper, inside and out. Place on a large sheet of heavy-duty foil in a large shallow baking pan.

Place 3 bacon slices lengthwise inside salmon. Stuff with lemon and onion slices. Place remaining bacon on top. Wrap foil to seal.

Bake 10 minutes per inch. Measure salmon at its thickest part (a large salmon may take a little longer). Test for doneness with a toothpick or knife tip. When opaque all the way through, it should be done. Discard bacon, lemon and onion.

Marinate
Broil

Serve with Almond Rice Pilaf, Steamed Green Beans and Sally Lunn Muffins.

Teriyaki Salmon Steaks

4   (6-oz) salmon steaks
¼   cup oil
2   tablespoons fresh lemon juice
2   tablespoons soy sauce
½   teaspoon dry mustard
½   teaspoon ground ginger

Place salmon in a sprayed 11x7-inch baking dish. Combine remaining ingredients; pour over top. Marinate 1 hour in refrigerator, turning occasionally.

Drain off marinade. Place salmon on rack in broiling pan. Broil 5 minutes, turn and broil 5 minutes more or until cooked through. Brush lightly with additional oil if salmon appears dry. Makes 4 servings.

Salmon Steak

4	salmon steaks, about 6 ounces each
2	tablespoons oil
2	tablespoons fresh lemon juice
1	small garlic clove, minced
2	tablespoons minced fresh basil

Pat salmon steaks dry with a paper towel and place on a broiler pan, skin-side down.

Combine remaining ingredients and brush some of the mixture over the salmon. Broil, about 8 to 10 minutes, or until steaks test done, basting once or twice with the sauce. You do not have to turn the steaks. Makes 4 servings.

Broil

Variation:
Substitute halibut for the salmon.

Easy Bake Parmesan Sole

4	fillet of sole
2	tablespoons butter
⅓	cup dry bread crumbs
2	tablespoons grated Parmesan cheese
1	teaspoon paprika

Rinse fillets and pat dry.

Combine remaining ingredients in a pie dish. Dip fillets in crumbs and place in a sprayed shallow baking pan. Bake 10 minutes or until fish flakes easily with a fork. If coating is dry, brush with a little melted butter. Makes 4 servings.

Oven 450°F

Serve with Hazelnut Asparagus, Oven Roasted New Potatoes and Caesar Salad.

Baked Halibut

Marinate
Oven 450°F

Serve with Brussels
Spout Sauté, Family
Favorite Rice Dish
and Garlic Bread.

3	tablespoons fresh lemon juice
1	teaspoon salt
½	teaspoon paprika
4	halibut steaks, 1-inch thick
½	cup chopped onion
2	tablespoons butter

In shallow dish, combine lemon juice, salt, and paprika. Add halibut, turning to coat. Marinate 1 hour, turning steaks after first half hour.

Meanwhile, sauté onion in butter until tender.

Place halibut in a sprayed 11x7-inch baking dish; top with onion mixture. Bake 10 minutes or until fish flakes easily with a fork. Makes 4 servings.

Favorite Halibut

Oven 450°F

This recipe is good
with almost any
white fish.

1	(1-lb) halibut, 1-inch thick
½	teaspoon garlic salt
3	tablespoons sour cream
1	green onion, chopped
2	tablespoons grated Parmesan cheese

Place halibut in a sprayed shallow baking dish. Sprinkle with garlic salt.

Combine sour cream and onion; spread over fish. Sprinkle with Parmesan. Bake 10 minutes or until cooked through. Makes 4 servings

Cheesy-Salsa Fish Fillet

Stove Top

4	fish fillets (perch, sole, etc.)
⅓	cup seasoned bread crumbs
1	tablespoon oil
¾	cup chunky salsa
4	slices Mozzarella cheese

Coat fillets with bread crumbs shaking off excess. Brown in oil in a medium skillet, turning once.

Top with salsa and cook through, topping each with a cheese slice toward end of cooking time. Makes 4 servings.

Try one of the new tropical salsas on the market; such as Peach Mango - delicious!

Tuna Rice Casserole

Oven 350°F

1	(6½-oz) can tuna, drained
1	(10¾-oz) can Cream of Mushroom soup
1	cup cooked rice
1	small onion, chopped
1	cup crushed potato chips

Gently combine ingredients until mixed. Spoon into a sprayed 1-quart casserole. If desired, top with additional crushed potato chips. Bake 30 to 45 minutes or until heated through. Makes 4 servings.

Serve with Crisp Green Salad and hot rolls.

"A lack of knowledge
about basic cookery
can be somewhat inconvenient."

James Beard

Jerk seasoning isn't for everyone, but it takes beautifully to grilled fish, pork, and chicken. Team with a fruity salsa. In case you are wondering, jerk seasoning is not the same as Cajun seasoning.

Jamaican Jerk Mahi-Mahi

4	(1-inch) mahi-mahi fillets or steaks
1	tablespoon oil
2	tablespoons Jamaican jerk seasoning

Lightly spray the grill rack. Place over medium-hot heat.

Brush mahi-mahi with oil. Sprinkle with seasoning and rub in. Grill fish, turning once, until opaque in the center, about 3 to 4 minutes per side. Makes 4 servings.

Note: Any firm white fish may be substituted for the mahi-mahi.

Stove Top

To make this a true piccata dish, you probably should add capers, but if you don't have a jar in your cupboard, you may not want to add them since they are quite expensive.

Scallop Piccata

1	teaspoon minced shallots
2	tablespoons butter, divided
4	ounces (10 to 15) bay scallops
2	tablespoons white wine
1	teaspoon lemon juice

In a medium skillet, sauté the shallots in 1 tablespoon butter. Add scallops and brown. Remove and keep warm.

Deglaze by adding the wine to the hot skillet and stirring quickly. Add lemon juice, then add the remaining butter and cook until slightly thickened. Return scallops and quickly heat through, if needed. Makes 2 servings.

Scallops & Ginger

1¼ pounds bay scallops
¼ cup butter
3 to 4 slices fresh ginger
   Salt and pepper

Rinse scallops and pat dry.

Heat butter in medium skillet. Add ginger and sauté briefly. Add scallops and continue to cook until scallops are heated through. Add salt and pepper to taste. Remove the ginger before serving. Makes 4 servings.

Baked Shrimp Scampi

2 pounds uncooked jumbo shrimp, peeled, deveined, butterflied
⅓ cup butter, melted
2 tablespoons olive oil
¼ cup fresh lemon juice
3 medium garlic cloves, minced

Place shrimp in a 13x9-inch baking dish. Combine remaining ingredients and pour over shrimp. Gently toss to coat. Spread evenly over pan and bake 6 to 10 minutes or until shrimp is pink and cooked through. Makes 4 servings.

Choose scallops that are pink or cream colored. Avoid the bright white ones that have probably been bleached in various preservatives.

Watch carefully. If the shrimp is overcooked, it will be tough.

Fresh crab can be substituted for the canned crab.

Crab Divan

1	(6½-oz) can crab, drained
2	cups broccoli florets, cooked
½	cup mayonnaise
1	teaspoon prepared mustard
1	tablespoon finely chopped onion
½	cup (2-oz) Cheddar cheese, shredded

Arrange broccoli in bottom of a sprayed 1-quart casserole. Distribute crab evenly over top.

Combine mayonnaise, mustard, and onion; spread over crab. Sprinkle with cheese. Bake 20 to 30 minutes or until heated through. Makes 4 servings.

Memories

The favorite meals we prepare for our family today will be fond memories when our children look back on their childhood.

Poultry

Tropical Chicken Kabobs

6	chicken breast halves, boned, skinned
1	(20-oz) can pineapple chunks
1	teaspoon ground ginger
1	orange bell pepper, cut into 1½-inch squares
1	onion, cut into 1½-inch squares
½	cup orange juice concentrate

Cut chicken into 1½-inch pieces and place in a large bowl. Open pineapple and drain juice over chicken pieces. Save pineapple for later. Add ginger to chicken and stir. Marinate at least 30 minutes.

On skewers, alternately thread chicken, pineapple, peppers and onions. Grill over medium heat, basting with orange juice concentrate, about 20 to 30 minutes or until cooked through.

Marinate
Grill

This is easy, colorful and delicious. A great company dish. Serve with rice pilaf, fresh asparagus and salad.

Italian Chicken Casserole

4	chicken breast halves, bone in
1	cup uncooked long-grain rice
1	(.65-oz) Italian salad dressing mix
2½	cups boiling water
1	(10¾-oz) can Cream of Chicken soup
	Salt and pepper

Spread rice in a sprayed 13x9-inch baking dish. Combine salad dressing mix, water and soup; mix well. Pour over rice. Place chicken, skin-side up, on top of rice. Sprinkle with salt and pepper. Cover dish with foil, and bake 60 minutes.

Remove foil and bake 20 to 30 minutes or until liquid is absorbed and chicken is tender. Makes 4 servings.

Oven 350°F

If doubling recipe, use two 13x9-inch baking dishes, not one large. For a more tender moist chicken, use bone-in chicken breast with skin.

An easy way to prepare chicken on those days when you have very little time to cook.

Lemon Pepper Chicken

4	chicken breasts halves
1	tablespoon olive oil
	Lemon pepper

Place chicken, skin-side up, on a shallow baking pan. Brush with oil. Sprinkle lightly with lemon pepper. Bake 40 to 50 minutes or until cooked through. Makes 4 servings.

Note: Decrease cooking time if using boneless chicken breasts.

Herb Chicken Bake

1	chicken, cut up
⅓	cup butter
1	can (10¾-oz) Cream of Chicken Soup with Herbs
1	(4-oz) can sliced mushrooms (optional)

Place chicken pieces, skin-side down, in a 13x9-inch baking dish. Slice butter and arrange on chicken. Bake 20 minutes. Turn chicken and bake 20 minutes.

Stir soup and mushrooms together; spoon over chicken. Bake 20 minutes or until chicken is cooked through. Makes 4 servings.

Entertaining

can be a lot of work, but you don't have to do everything. People love to contribute, so take them up on it. Have them bring an appetizer, salad, side dish or dessert. You won't be so rushed and you can also enjoy the party. Besides, it's always fun to try everyone else's favorite dishes.

Baked Fried Chicken

8   chicken legs
      Salt and pepper
      Paprika
6   tablespoons butter

Sprinkle chicken with salt, pepper, and paprika. Place, skin-side down, in a shallow baking pan. Dot with butter. Cover with foil and bake 30 minutes.

Remove foil. Increase temperature to 425°, bake 30 minutes or until cooked through. Makes 4 servings.

Oven 400°F

The easiest way there is to "fry" chicken. Serve with mashed potatoes, gravy, green beans, Jiffy Cornbread Muffins.

Chicken–Vegetable Dish

4   chicken breast halves, skinned, boned
      Salt and pepper
2   tablespoons oil
1¼   cups chicken broth
2   cups broccoli florets
1   medium yellow squash, sliced

Sprinkle chicken with salt and pepper. Heat oil in a large skillet and brown chicken on both sides. Add chicken broth; cover and cook 15 to 20 minutes or until chicken is cooked through.

Add vegetables and sprinkle lightly with salt and pepper. Cover and cook 5 to 6 minutes or until vegetables are just crisp-tender. Makes 4 servings

Stove Top

No More Dry Grilled Chicken

Grilled chicken is sometimes a little drier than we would like it to be. If this should happen, combine ¼ cup honey and ½ teaspoon dry mustard and brush over chicken just before serving.

Serve with white rice to soak up the delicious cream sauce.

Golden Chicken Bake

1	chicken, cut up
⅓	cup butter
1	(10¾-oz) can Cream of Chicken soup
1	teaspoon minced dried parsley

Arrange chicken, skin-side down, in a 13x9-inch baking dish. Place dabs of butter over chicken. Bake 20 minutes. Turn chicken and bake 20 minutes.

Stir soup and pour over chicken. Sprinkle with parsley. Bake 20 minutes more. Makes 4 to 6 servings.

Rush Hour Chicken

Purchase a roasted chicken at your favorite supermarket along with deli potato salad and/or other salads of your choice. Add hot bread or rolls and serve with pride. If you have a little more time, cook some potatoes for mashed potatoes, and while that is cooking, make chicken gravy using the drippings from the chicken. Serve with steamed green beans and canned refrigerator biscuits.

Hawaiian Chicken

4	(each) chicken legs, thighs and breasts
1	(6-oz) can frozen orange juice, thawed
2	tablespoons butter, melted
2	(8-oz) cans crushed pineapple, with juice
1½	teaspoons ground ginger
1	tablespoon soy sauce

Place chicken pieces, skin-side up, in a roasting pan. The one that came with your oven is just about the right size.

Combine remaining ingredients. Pour over chicken and bake about 60 minutes or until chicken is cooked through, basting frequently. Makes 6 to 8 servings.

Chicken Broccoli Casserole

Oven 350°F

1	(20-oz) package frozen chopped broccoli
5	cups cooked long-grain rice
2½	cups cubed cooked chicken
2	(10¾-oz) cans Cream of Chicken Soup
1	cup mayonnaise
2	cups (8-oz) Mozzarella cheese, shredded, divided

Place frozen broccoli in a colander and run under hot water; drain thoroughly. Spread on bottom of a sprayed 13x9-inch baking dish. Spoon rice over top.

Combine chicken, soup, mayonnaise and 1 cup of the cheese. Pour over rice. Sprinkle with remaining cheese. (Dish will be quite full.) Bake 30 to 35 minutes or until heated through. Watch carefully last few minutes. Cover with foil if cheese is browning too fast. Makes 8 servings.

This delightful dish features a combination of favorite ingredients made even better by the addition of a special tossed green salad and toasted French bread. This is a large recipe and should be baked in a deep 13x9-inch baking pan or dish.

Savory Grilled Chicken

1	chicken, cut up
	Seasoned salt
	Butter, melted

Place chicken on a large piece of heavy-duty foil. Sprinkle generously with salt. Fold foil over and secure tightly. Place on grill and cook 45 minutes, turning frequently, to avoid burning. Remove chicken from foil and place directly on grill, turning to brown both sides. Baste with butter. Meat is so tender it will literally fall off the bone. Makes 4 servings.

Chicken Kabobs

Boneless
Chicken cubes
Oil
Apricot preserves

Thread chicken pieces onto skewers. Brush lightly with oil. Cook over medium hot grill, turning to cook all sides. Brush with apricot preserves last few minutes of cooking time.

Creamy Chicken Almond

1	chicken, cut up
⅓	cup flour
1	teaspoon lemon pepper
2	tablespoons vegetable oil
1	(10¾-oz) can Cream of Chicken soup
⅓	cup slivered almonds

Rinse chicken and pat dry. Combine flour and pepper. Coat chicken with flour, shaking off excess.

Heat oil in a large skillet and brown chicken on both sides. Place, skin-side up, in a sprayed 13x9-inch baking dish.

Stir soup, then spread over chicken pieces. Sprinkle with almonds. Bake 50 to 60 minutes or until chicken is cooked through and tender. Makes 4 servings.

Roast Chicken

1	(3 to 4-lb) chicken
1	tablespoon oil
	Paprika

Clean chicken and wipe dry. Place on rack in baking pan. Brush with oil and sprinkle with paprika.

Bake 1 to 1½ hours or until temperature reaches 170°. Let stand 10 minutes before serving.

Panko Chicken Dijon

Oven 375°F

4	chicken breast halves, skinned and boned
4	tablespoons melted butter, divided
1½	tablespoons Dijon mustard
3	tablespoons grated Parmesan cheese
½	cup Panko breading

Wash chicken and pat dry. Combine 3 tablespoons of the butter with the mustard in a small shallow dish. It may look curdled, but that's okay.

Combine Parmesan and Panko in a flat dish. Dip chicken in butter mixture, then in crumb mixture, coating both sides. Place on sprayed shallow baking pan. Brush with remaining tablespoon butter. Bake 30 to 40 minutes or until cooked through and golden. Makes 4 servings.

Serve with Dijon Mustard Sauce made by mixing equal parts of Dijon mustard and mayonnaise.

Note: Panko is a crunchy Japanese style breading found in the Asian department of most supermarkets.

Peachy Chicken

Oven 350°F

1	chicken, cut up
1	(29-oz) can peach halves, save juice
¼	cup soy sauce

Arrange chicken, skin-side down, in a sprayed 13x9-inch baking dish. Combine peach syrup with soy sauce. Pour over chicken. Bake 30 minutes.

Turn and bake 20 minutes or until cooked through, basting frequently. Serve with peaches. Makes 4 servings.

If desired, peach halves can be heated along with chicken the last 10 minutes of baking time.

Quick Chicken Divan

1	pound fresh broccoli, cooked
4	large slices cooked chicken or turkey
1	(10¾-oz) can Cream of Chicken soup
⅓	cup milk
½	cup (2-oz) Cheddar cheese, shredded

Place broccoli in a sprayed 11x7-inch baking dish. Top with chicken.

Combine soup and milk until blended. Pour over chicken. Sprinkle with cheese. Bake 30 minutes or until heated through. Makes 4 servings.

Oven 350°F

Serve with Romaine Artichoke Salad and Quick Focaccia Bread.

Sweet-Sour Chicken

1	chicken, cut up
1	cup ketchup
¾	cup white vinegar
1½	teaspoons prepared mustard
1½	cups firmly packed brown sugar

Rinse chicken and pat dry.

Combine remaining ingredients in a small saucepan. Bring to a boil; reduce heat and simmer 30 minutes.

Place chicken, skin-side down, in a sprayed 13x9-inch baking dish. Brush generously with sauce. Bake 30 minutes; turn and bake 20 to 30 minutes, basting frequently with the sauce. Makes 4 servings.

Oven 350°F

A nice sweet-sour sauce flavors this easy chicken recipe. Serve with rice to absorb all the wonderful sauce.

Garlic Butter Chicken

Oven 350°F

1	chicken, cut up
½	cup butter
1	tablespoon garlic salt
¼	teaspoon pepper

Place chicken, skin-side down, in a sprayed 13x9-inch baking dish.

Combine remaining ingredients. Brush chicken with some of the mixture and bake 30 minutes, basting twice. Turn chicken and bake 20 to 30 minutes or until cooked through, basting frequently. Makes 4 to 6 servings.

Serve with Oven Roasted New Potatoes and Best Ever Broccoli.

Company Chicken

Stove Top

4	chicken breast halves, skinned, boned
¼	cup flour
2	tablespoons oil
2	slices deli ham, halved
2	slices Monterey Jack cheese, halved

Dip chicken in flour; shake off excess. Pour oil in medium skillet and heat over medium-high heat. Add chicken and cook until cooked through, turning once.

Top with a slice of ham and then the cheese. Cook until cheese is melted. Makes 4 servings.

For a tropical twist, you can place a sliced pineapple ring between the ham and cheese slices.

Orange Almond Chicken

6	large chicken breast halves, skinned
	Salt and pepper
¾	cup flour
3	oranges (you will need ¾ cup orange juice and 1½ teaspoons orange peel)
6	tablespoons butter
6	tablespoons sliced almonds

Sprinkle chicken with salt and pepper. Coat with flour. Place in 13x9-inch baking dish, skin-side up.

Combine juice and orange peel; pour over chicken. Dot chicken with butter. Sprinkle with almonds. Bake 45 to 60 minutes, basting 2 or 3 times. Makes 6 servings.

Note: If using boneless chicken breasts, cooking time will be less.

Bernstein's Baked Chicken

1	chicken, cut up
¼	cup Bernstein's Cheese Fantastico Dressing

I hope your supermarket carries Bernstein dressings. They can be used in many wonderful chicken recipes, as well as in your favorite salad combinations.

Brush chicken with dressing. Place, skin-side up, in a sprayed 13x9-inch baking dish. Bake 45 to 60 minutes, basting once or twice with dressing until chicken is golden and cooked through. Makes 4 to 6 servings.

Pesto Stuffed Chicken

4	large chicken breasts, with skin
4	tablespoons pesto sauce
1	tablespoon oil
½	cup grated Parmesan cheese

Spread pesto under chicken skin, leaving skin attached. Place in a sprayed 13x9-inch baking dish. Brush with oil and bake 30 minutes.

Brush with drippings and sprinkle with cheese. Bake 10 to 15 minutes or until cooked through. Makes 4 servings.

Shopper's Chicken

6	chicken breast halves
1	cup sour cream
2	tablespoons lemon juice
1	teaspoon salt
1	teaspoon paprika
½	cup butter

Place chicken, skin-side up, in a sprayed 13x9-inch baking dish.

Combine remaining ingredients, except butter, and spread over chicken. Dot with butter. Bake 30 to 40 minutes or until cooked through. Makes 6 servings.

Oven 350°F

Use your favorite homemade or purchased pesto sauce.

Oven 350°F

Chicken breast halves come in so many different sizes which can affect the cooking time. Chicken with the bone in takes longer than boneless pieces. Also, bear in mind that frozen boneless chicken breasts are usually quite a bit thinner than the fresh and may take very little time to cook. If your chicken is dry and tough, you may be overcooking it.

Asian Glazed Chicken

Oven 350°F

This recipe imparts a lot of flavor for so few ingredients.

4	chicken breast halves
2	tablespoons butter, melted
2	tablespoons Worcestershire sauce
1	tablespoon soy sauce

Line a shallow baking pan with foil for easier cleaning. Place chicken on foil, skin-side up.

Combine remaining ingredients. Brush chicken and bake 30 to 40 minutes, basting occasionally. Makes 4 servings.

Ben's Chicken Parmesan

Oven 350°F

My grandson, Ben, loves to be the taste tester for new recipes. He ate 2 servings of this one.

4	chicken breast halves, skinned, boned
3	tablespoons grated Parmesan cheese
1¼	cups spaghetti sauce
1	cup (4-oz) Mozzarella cheese, shredded Parsley

Place chicken in a sprayed 11x7-inch baking dish.

Combine Parmesan and spaghetti sauce; pour over chicken. Cover. Bake 30 minutes or until cooked through.

Top with cheese and a sprinkle of parsley. Bake 5 minutes to melt cheese. Makes 4 servings.

Chicken & Coconut

Oven 350°F

4	chicken breasts, halved, skinned, boned
	Salt and pepper
	Oil
⅓	cup fine dry bread crumbs
⅓	cup flaked coconut
¼	cup butter, melted

Serve with Almond Rice Pilaf, Broccoli Meringue and Sweet-Sour Spinach Salad.

Sprinkle chicken with salt and pepper. Brush with oil.

Combine bread crumbs and coconut. Roll chicken in mixture to coat. Place in a sprayed 13x9-inch dish; drizzle with melted butter. Bake 30 to 40 minutes or until tender. Makes 4 servings.

Chicken & Noodles

Stove Top

3	cups chicken broth
1½	cups (4-oz) medium egg noodles
2	cups fresh broccoli florets
2	cups cubed cooked chicken (or turkey)
¼	teaspoon lemon pepper
½	cup sour cream

This recipe is very easy and very fast. If you have some leftover chicken or turkey, this dish can be made in less than 15 minutes.

Heat chicken broth in a 2 quart saucepan; bring to a boil. Add noodles and cook about 4 minutes; stirring occasionally. Add broccoli; cover and continue cooking 4 minutes. Add chicken and lemon pepper; cook about 4 minutes or until heated through and broccoli is just crisp-tender.

At this point you probably have very little liquid left in the pan, but this needs to be drained off. Stir in sour cream and cook, over low heat, until heated through. Makes 4 servings.

Chicken Marmalade

1	chicken, cut up
¼	cup butter, melted
1	cup orange marmalade
¼	cup packed brown sugar
½	teaspoon dry ginger

Place chicken, skin-side down, in a sprayed 13x9-inch baking dish. Brush with butter. Bake 15 minutes. Turn chicken, baste with butter, and bake 15 minutes.

Combine remaining ingredients and brush on chicken. Bake 20 minutes or until tender and richly glazed, basting frequently. Makes 4 servings.

Stove Top

Variations:

• Pineapple slices, cooked broccoli spears, Monterey Jack cheese

• Sliced tomatoes, cooked broccoli spears, Mozzarella cheese

• Sliced ham, cooked asparagus spears, Swiss cheese

Company Swiss Chicken

4	chicken breast halves, skinned and boned
2	tablespoons oil
1	(6½-oz) jar marinated artichoke hearts, drained
4	slices Swiss cheese

Place each chicken breast between plastic wrap and pound to ¼-inch thickness. Heat oil in a large skillet. Add chicken and cook 6 to 8 minutes or until cooked through, turning once.

Arrange artichokes on top of chicken; top with a slice of cheese (trim if too large). Cover skillet and cook until cheese is melted. Makes 4 servings.

Quick Chicken Mozzarella

Use desired amounts of the following ingredients:

Frozen breaded chicken breast patties
Mozzarella cheese slices
Prepared spaghetti or pizza sauce

Cook chicken patties as directed on package using a medium skillet and cooking on top of stove.

Place a cheese slice on top of each patty. Pour desired amount of sauce around the patties and heat through.

Sweet Pepper Chicken

4	chicken breast halves, skinned and boned
¼	cup white vinegar
½	cup firmly packed brown sugar
1	(20-oz) can pineapple chunks, save juice
2	tablespoons cornstarch
2	bell peppers, ½ red pepper and ½ green pepper, cut into narrow strips

Cut chicken into bite-size pieces. Cook over medium-high heat in a sprayed nonstick skillet, until cooked through, stirring frequently. Set aside. In medium saucepan, combine vinegar and brown sugar with ½ *cup water*. Bring to a boil; reduce heat. Drain pineapple. Combine cornstarch with pineapple juice; mix until blended. Stir into saucepan. Add pineapple and peppers. Cook, over low heat, until sauce has thickened and peppers are crisp-tender. Makes 6 servings.

Stove Top

After a soccer game - this is perfect.

Stove Top

This is colorful, delicious and low calorie. Serve over rice.

Turkey Roasting
Guaranteed Success

Defrost Fresh or frozen - it's up to you. Fresh turkey is a little bit higher priced, but it will not take days of refrigerator space to thaw. The safest recommended method to thaw turkey is in the refrigerator. Allow 24 hours for each 5 pounds. For example, a 15-pound turkey will take 3 days to thaw. If you are running tight on space or time, an alternative method is to thaw the turkey in cold water. Allow approximately 30 minutes per pound, and change water every hour or two.

Prepare When turkey is thawed, you may prepare it for roasting. First, be sure to remove the paper sack inside of the turkey containing the giblets. Remove any other pieces, such as the neck, that may be inside the turkey. Next, rinse the turkey both inside and out. Dry with paper towels. (Be sure to thoroughly clean all surfaces that have come into contact with the raw turkey.)

Safety First It is now recommended that poultry not be stuffed with dressing, but rather the dressing be baked separately in a casserole dish or even a slow cooker. However, if you still insist on stuffing your bird, the dressing must reach an internal temperature of 165°F thus killing any harmful bacteria. (Do not pack the dressing, but spoon in lightly.) But, reaching this safe temperature may cause the breast meat to be overcooked and dry.

Be Sure To test for doneness, an instant read thermometer should read 170°F when inserted into the thickest part of the thigh. When done, remove from oven, cover with foil and let stand 30-60 minutes before carving. (If allowing to stand more than 30 minutes, remove from oven when temperature reaches 165°. Meat will continue to cook and meat will be moist.. Slicing any meat right out of the oven, will cause the juice to run and the meat to be dry

Traditional Method - Bake at 325°F

Place turkey, breast-side up, in shallow baking pan. Brush with oil or butter.

POUNDS	HOURS	REMOVE FROM OVEN WHEN TEMPERATURE REACHES:
8-12	$2\frac{1}{4}$-$2\frac{3}{4}$	170°F (thigh)
12-16	$2\frac{3}{4}$-$3\frac{1}{4}$	170°F (thigh)
16-20	$3\frac{1}{4}$-$3\frac{3}{4}$	170°F (thigh)
20-24	$3\frac{3}{4}$-$4\frac{1}{2}$	170°F (thigh)

Foil Wrapped Method - Bake at 425°F
(Faster than traditional)

Using wide, heavy-duty foil, cut 2 long strips. Place one piece lengthwise in a large shallow roasting pan and one piece crosswise in pan. Place turkey, breast side up, on top of foil. Brush with oil or butter. Bring 2 opposite ends of foil up over turkey; fold ends together to seal. Bring remaining two ends of foil up and seal. Bake at 450°F. (To brown turkey, open foil during the last 30 minutes of cooking time.)

Pounds	Hours	REMOVE FROM OVEN WHEN TEMPERATURE REACHES:
8-12	$1\frac{1}{4}$-2	170°F (thigh)
12-16	2-$2\frac{1}{4}$	170°F (thigh)
16-20	$2\frac{1}{4}$-$2\frac{1}{2}$	170°F (thigh)
20-24	$2\frac{1}{2}$-$2\frac{3}{4}$	170°F (thigh)

A wonderful mar-
malade glaze with
a touch of black
pepper.

Orange Glazed Turkey Breast

1	(6-lb) whole turkey breast
2	teaspoons oil
⅓	cup orange marmalade
1	tablespoon prepared mustard
2	teaspoons Worcestershire sauce
½	teaspoon cracked pepper

Place turkey breast, breast-side up, on a rack in a roasting pan. Brush with oil. Cover with foil and bake 1½ to 2 hours.

Combine remaining ingredients and brush over turkey. Cook 30 to 40 minutes or until temperature reaches 160°, basting frequently with the pan drippings. Cover with foil and let stand 15 minutes before slicing. Makes about 12 servings.

No matter how care-
ful we are, we always
have some leftovers
after that big turkey
dinner - at least I
hope we do. This isn't
anything fancy, but
it is easy, quick and
does use up some of
those leftovers.

Oh So Easy Turkey Dinner

4	cups leftover stuffing
8	slices turkey or enough to cover stuffing
1½	cups whole berry cranberry sauce
2	cups gravy, heated

Layer ingredients in order given in a sprayed 7x11-inch baking dish.

Cover with foil and bake 25 to 30 minutes or until heated through. Makes 6 servings.

Note: Amounts can vary somewhat according to the size of turkey slices or how much you have. If the stuffing is dry you may want to use more gravy.

Pasta

Buttered Cheesy Pasta

12	ounces spaghetti
½	cup butter, sliced
½	cup grated Parmesan cheese
	Freshly ground black pepper, to taste

Cook pasta according to package directions. Quickly rinse, drain, and return to pot.

Add butter and toss to melt. Add Parmesan and pepper and toss until cheese is melted. Makes 6 servings.

Stove Top

This makes a great side dish with your favorite meats.

Stove Top Macaroni & Cheese

1½	cups (6-oz) elbow macaroni
¾	cup heavy cream
2	light dashes nutmeg (not too much)
3	tablespoons grated Parmesan cheese

Cook macaroni according to package directions. Rinse and drain thoroughly. Pour into a medium saucepan. Add cream, ¾ *cup water*, and nutmeg. Bring to a boil and cook over medium heat, about 6 to 8 minutes or until liquid is absorbed, stirring frequently.

Pour into a sprayed 8x8-inch baking dish and sprinkle with Parmesan cheese. Place under a pre-heated broiler and broil just until cheese is golden. Makes 6 servings.

Stove Top Broil

A flavorful twist on traditional macaroni and cheese.

I could make a whole meal out of this dish. The chewy cheese is a nice contrast to the creamy pasta.

Baked Pasta & Cream

8	ounces penne
1	cup heavy cream, divided
1	cup (4-oz) Mozzarella cheese, softened
2	tablespoons grated Parmesan cheese

Cook pasta according to package directions; rinse and drain.

Meanwhile, heat ½ cup of the cream in a large saucepan. Add pasta and cook, stirring frequently until cream is absorbed.

Sprinkle half the Mozzarella cheese in a sprayed 8x8-inch baking dish. Add half the pasta, remaining cheese, then remaining pasta. Pour remaining cream over top. Sprinkle with Parmesan cheese. Bake 25 to 30 minutes or until most of the liquid is absorbed. Let stand 5 minutes. Makes 6 servings.

Serve this versatile dish topped with shrimp, crab, or chicken.

Pasta with Brie & Shrimp

8	ounces linguine
8	ounces Brie cheese, diced
½	cup whipping cream
2	tablespoons finely chopped parsley
	Freshly ground pepper to taste
8	ounces cooked shrimp (should be hot)

Cook pasta according to package directions. Rinse and drain thoroughly. Return to pot and add Brie, stirring to melt. Add cream, parsley, and pepper.

Place on serving plate and top with shrimp. Makes 6 servings.

Note: Crust should be removed from Brie before dicing.

Cheese Ravioli

2	packages (9-oz each) cheese-filled ravioli
2	tablespoons butter
1	large garlic clove, minced
1	tablespoon chopped fresh parsley
1	cup heavy whipping cream
¼	cup grated Asiago or Parmesan cheese

Stove Top
Broil

Serve with chicken or salmon.

In large pot, cook pasta according to directions on package.

Meanwhile, just before pasta is ready, melt butter in a small skillet. Add garlic and parsley and quickly cook over medium-low heat (you don't want the garlic to brown).

Drain pasta and rinse with cold water. Return to pot; add garlic mixture and cream. Cook on low heat until cream is reduced slightly, about 3 to 4 minutes. Place in a sprayed 11 x 7-inch baking dish and sprinkle with cheese. Place under broiler and broil until cheese is melted and lightly browned. Makes 6 side dishes or 4 main dishes.

Linguine with Mascarpone

16	ounces linguine
1	(8-oz) container Mascarpone cheese, softened
¼	cup parsley
½	cup grated Parmesan cheese

Stove Top

These convenient "on hand" ingredients can be thrown together for a quick, yet delectable meal. Does reheat nicely in the microwave.

Cook pasta according to package directions. Rinse and drain. Return to pot.

Add Mascarpone cheese and parsley. Place on serving plates and sprinkle with Parmesan. Makes 8 servings

Serve with Crisp
Green Salad and
Cheesy Quick Bread.

Spinach–Tomato Tortellini

1	tablespoon olive oil
1	large garlic clove, minced
2	(14.5-oz) cans whole Italian style tomatoes, cut up
1	tablespoon sugar
1	(8-oz) package spinach tortellini with cheese

Heat oil in a medium saucepan. Add garlic and cook about 2 minutes, but do not brown. Add tomatoes (do not drain); and sugar. Bring to a boil; reduce heat and simmer about 45 minutes or until thickened.

Meanwhile, cook tortellini according to directions on package. Drain and rinse thoroughly. Place tortellini on a large serving platter and top with some of the tomato sauce. Makes 4 servings.

The Spaghetti Factory restaurants serve this delicious pasta. This is my daughter's version and is equally as good.

Browned Butter & Myzithra Cheese

8	ounces spaghetti
⅓	cup butter
2	medium garlic cloves, minced
½	cup grated Myzithra cheese

Cook pasta according to directions on package; drain.

Meanwhile, in a small skillet, melt butter over medium-low heat. Add garlic and cook until butter turns a light brown. Watch carefully at this point. If it turns too dark, it will have to be discarded. Add to pasta and toss to coat. Place on individual serving dishes and sprinkle with about 2 tablespoons cheese. Makes 4 side-dish servings or 2 main dish servings.

Baked Salmon & Pasta

8	ounces linguine
4	(6-oz) salmon fillets
1	tablespoon butter, melted
	Salt and pepper
¼	cup pesto, or to taste

Cook pasta according to package directions. Rinse and drain.

Meanwhile, place salmon in a sprayed shallow baking pan. Brush with butter. Sprinkle with salt and pepper. Bake 8 to 10 minutes or until cooked through.

Toss pasta with pesto. Spoon onto a large serving platter and arrange fillets over top. Makes 4 servings.

Stove Top
Oven 450°F

Pesto and salmon are a great flavor combination.
If desired, grill the salmon and serve the pasta on the side.

Fettuccine Alfredo

16	ounces fettuccine
½	cup butter, melted
1	cup heavy whipping cream
1	cup freshly grated Parmesan cheese
	Salt and pepper

Cook pasta as directed on package; drain. Return pasta to pan. Add butter, cream and cheese. Add salt and pepper. Toss over low heat until pasta is coated and mixture is heated through. Makes 4 servings.

Stove Top

Quick Pasta Sauce

Cook heavy whipping cream until thickened. Pour over pasta and toss. This works nicely as a side-dish pasta and for simple pasta dishes with a cream sauce.

Serve with toasted bread triangles, your favorite salad and fruit for dessert.

Chicken Linguine

8	ounces linguine
4	chicken breast halves, skinned, boned
1	tablespoon oil
½	cup chopped green onion
1	cup whipping cream
½	cup grated Parmesan cheese

Cook pasta according to package directions. Rinse and drain.

Meanwhile, slice chicken crosswise into narrow strips. Toss with oil. Add to a heated large skillet and cook over medium heat until cooked through, adding onions during last couple minutes of cooking time. (May have to cook chicken in 2 batches.)

Add cream and cook 4 to 5 minutes or until slightly thickened. Add Parmesan and cook until melted. Place pasta on plates and top with chicken mixture. Makes 6 servings.

Company Menu

Chicken Linguine

Brie Salad

Tomato-Garlic Pizza Bread

Purchased cheesecake with

choice of toppings

Kid's Corner

Apple Peanut Butter Discs

1	apple, such as Gala, Fuji, or Golden Delicious
2	tablespoons peanut butter

Wash apple and pat dry with a paper towel. Core the apple (you may need Mom for this part). Fill center with peanut butter. Wrap in plastic wrap or foil and chill about 30 minutes. When ready to eat, cut crosswise into ½-inch slices.

Popcorn Balls

¼	cup butter
½	teaspoon vanilla extract
1	(10½-oz) package marshmallows
6	quarts popped popcorn

Combine butter, vanilla, and marshmallows in top of a double boiler. Stir until melted and smooth.

Pour over popcorn and mix well. Butter hands and form into balls, but be careful, mixture may be hot. Makes 12 to 15 balls.

Children's Bird Seed

2	cups Corn Pops® cereal
½	cup raisins
½	cup peanuts
½	cup M&M® candies

Combine ingredients in large bowl. Makes 3½ cups.

Chill

These apple slices and a glass of milk make a great after school snack.

Stove Top

Great Idea:

Mold popcorn balls around the straight end of a candy cane. Wrap with plastic wrap, tie with a ribbon, and hang on your Christmas tree. Give to your friends and family on Christmas day.

A great school snack when it's your turn to provide the treat.

Pumpkin Seed Snacks

2   cups fresh pumpkin seeds
1   tablespoon vegetable oil
1   tablespoon butter, melted
    Salt

Wipe fibers from pumpkin seeds, but do not wash. Place in a medium bowl.

Combine oil and melted butter. Pour over seeds and toss to coat. Spread out on a large baking sheet. Sprinkle lightly with salt.

Place baking sheet in oven and bake 30 minutes or until golden in color and crisp. Remove from oven and let cool. Store in covered container. Makes 2 cups.

Stove Top
Chill

Surprise your friends with these delightful treats.

Butterscotch Crunchies

1   cup butterscotch chips
½   cup peanut butter
2   cups (3-oz can) Chow Mein Noodles
1   cup miniature marshmallows

Melt butterscotch chips and peanut butter in top of double boiler; stir to blend. Remove from heat.

Gently stir in noodles and marshmallows. Drop by teaspoon onto a baking sheet. Chill in refrigerator until set. Makes 3 dozen.

> Before assembling, read
> through the entire recipe first.

Peanut Butter Bars

1   cup semi-sweet chocolate chips
⅓   cup peanut butter
4   cups Cocoa Krispies®

Melt chocolate chips in top of double boiler. Stir in peanut butter. Remove from heat. Gently stir in Cocoa Krispies.

Press mixture into a sprayed 8x8-inch baking dish. Let cool and then cut into bars. Makes 3 dozen.

Stove Top

You may want to double the recipe and use a 13x9-inch baking dish.

Peanut Butter Cupcakes

1   (18.25-oz) box yellow cake mix
1   cup creamy peanut butter
1⅓   cups water
3   large eggs
½   cup mini semi-sweet chocolate chips
1   (16-oz) can chocolate frosting

In large mixer bowl, combine first 4 ingredients following mixing directions on box. Stir in chocolate chips.

Spoon batter into sprayed muffin tins, filling ⅔ full. Bake 18 to 20 minutes or until center tests done. Remove from muffin tins and let cool on rack. Spread with frosting. Makes 12 to 18 cupcakes, depending on the size of the muffin tins.

Oven 350°F

These are quite rich and are equally as good with or without frosting.

Quick Coconut Cookies

Oven 350°F

Keep the ingredients on hand and kids can make these for snacks or treats.

1	(18.25-oz) box white cake mix
⅓	cup oil
2	large eggs
½	cup dried cranberries
1	cup flaked coconut

In mixer bowl, combine first 3 ingredients; mix until blended. Add remaining ingredients and beat just until mixed through.

Drop in mounds, about the size of a walnut, onto a cookie sheet. Bake 10 to 12 minutes or until slightly soft in center and light golden brown. Cool on rack. Makes 36 to 42 cookies.

Pretty in Pink Cake

Oven 350°F

You will be impressed by how tall this cake is and how easy it is to make.

1	(16-oz) box Angel food cake mix
¼	cup presweetened cherry Kool-Aid®

In mixer bowl, place cake mix and Kool-Aid. Prepare cake as directed on box using a 10-inch Angel food cake tube pan. Follow directions very carefully. The only other ingredient you have to add is water, as directed on the package.

Pour into ungreased Angel food cake pan and bake as directed on package. Makes 12 servings.

To Serve: You can serve the cake by itself or with a serving of fruit or ice cream. A dollop of whipped cream sprinkled with coconut is very good too.

Easy Oatmeal Cookies

Oven 350°F

1   cup butter
1   cup firmly packed brown sugar
1   cup flour
1   teaspoon baking soda
2   cups quick-cooking oats

Cream butter and sugar in mixer bowl. Add flour and baking soda and beat until mixed. Stir in oats. Roll into 1-inch balls. Place on an ungreased baking sheet and press slightly. Bake 8 to 10 minutes. Makes 4 dozen.

Let the youngest children roll the cookies and place them on a cookie sheet.

Frozen Fudgesicles

Freeze

1   (3.9-oz) box instant chocolate pudding mix
2   cups milk
¼   cup sugar
1   cup canned evaporated milk

In large mixer bowl, combine pudding and the 2 cups of milk. Beat 2 minutes with mixer and watch carefully as it might splatter on you.

Stir in sugar and canned milk. Pour immediately into popsicle molds. Freeze. Makes about 12 to 14 Fudgesicles.

Believe it or not, these are much better than store bought. Always make more than you think you need. The grown ups like them almost as much as the kids do.

Popsicles

Freeze

Variation:
Add fresh or frozen raspberries, blueberries, or sliced strawberries.

1   (0.17-oz) package unsweetened Kool-Aid®, any flavor
1   cup sugar
4   cups water

Combine all the ingredients in a large pitcher. Stir until the sugar is dissolved. Pour into popsicle molds and freeze. Makes about 18 popsicles, depending on the size of the molds.

Raspberry Smoothie

Blender

Nutritious and delicious.

1   (10-oz) package frozen sweetened raspberries, thawed
2   cups orange juice
½   cup milk
6   ice cubes

Place ingredients in blender and process until smooth. Makes 4½ cups.

Lemon Julius Smoothie

Blender

Make this for all of your friends for a refreshing summer treat.

1   (6-oz) can frozen lemonade concentrate
1   (6-oz) can frozen orange juice concentrate
2   cups vanilla ice cream

Combine ingredients in blender along with *4 cups water*; blend on medium speed until mixed and foamy. If blender is too small to hold all the ingredients, make half the recipe at a time and combine the two mixes. Makes 7½ cups.

Yummy Hot Dogs

1	(8-oz) can refrigerated Crescent rolls
4	teaspoons melted butter
4	teaspoons prepared mustard
8	hot dogs

Separate crescents into 8 rolls. Brush each with melted butter and spread with mustard. Place hot dog on wide end and roll towards narrow end.

Place on ungreased baking sheet. Brush with melted butter and bake 12 to 14 minutes or until rolls are lightly browned. Makes 8 servings.

Oven 375°F

Variation:
Substitute flour tortillas for the crescent rolls.

Easy Parmesan Knots

1	(11-oz) can refrigerated breadsticks
3	tablespoons butter
1	tablespoon grated Parmesan cheese
¼	teaspoon garlic salt
½	teaspoon dried parsley

Unroll breadsticks and separate. Tie each breadstick into a loose knot (remember the bread will get bigger when it bakes) and place on a baking sheet. Bake 10 to 12 minutes or until golden.

While rolls are baking, place butter in a small microwave safe bowl and microwave until melted. Stir in the Parmesan cheese, garlic salt, and parsley. Brush butter mixture over each baked roll.

Put rolls in a pretty basket or dish and serve hot. Makes 12 rolls.

Oven 375°F

Easy Clean-Up

Pack a handy-wipe in a plastic bag. It can be used for cleaning hands before and after school lunches. This is especially great for field trip days when washing facilities may not be available.

Hot Dogs & Breadsticks

Oven 350°F

Have your friends over and impress them with lunch. Serve with fresh fruit and Peanut Butter Bars.

1	**(11-oz) can refrigerated breadstick dough**
12	**hot dogs**

Open package and unroll dough. Separate into 12 strips.

Wrap one strip around each hot dog, stretching a little, if necessary, to wrap around three times with both ends tucked under bottom of the hot dog. Place on a baking sheet.

Bake 12 to 15 minutes or until lightly browned.

Tip: If desired, use as many hot dogs as needed. If you don't need 12 hot dogs, twist remaining breadstick dough and place on baking sheet. Sprinkle with poppy seeds or garlic salt and bake along with the hot dogs.

Quick Lunch Meal

Stove Top

Surprise Mom and tell her you will fix lunch.

1	**(15-oz) can baked beans**
1	**(11-oz) can Mexicorn, drained**
¼	**cup ketchup**
6	**hot dogs, sliced**

In small saucepan, combine all the ingredients and heat through. Makes 4 to 6 servings.

Mealtime

Meal time is when kids sit down to continue eating.

Kid's Favorite Flank Steak

1   flank steak
¼   cup soy sauce, approximately

Pour enough soy sauce in a shallow dish to cover bottom. Add flank steak and marinate 60 minutes, turning steak frequently.

Remove from marinade and broil or grill. Do not overcook, as this tends to toughen the meat. Slice crosswise into narrow strips. Makes 4 servings.

Marinate
Broil or Grill

Simple and delicious. For variety, add ¼ cup pineapple juice. An adult may need to help you with this recipe.

Super Safety Rule

Raw meat can carry harmful germs and bacteria. You must be careful when handling any raw meat. Be sure to wash your hands and anything that touches the meat or its juices with hot soapy water.

After marinating meat, the liquid should be discarded.

If you want to use some of the marinade for basting the meat while it is cooking, set aside a few tablespoons before pouring marinade over raw meat.

You can really impress your friends by serving this colorful and tasty pizza.

Paulina's Veggie Pesto Pizza

1	purchased 12-inch baked pizza crust
½	cup pesto
1½	cups (6-oz) Mozzarella cheese, shredded
¾	cup broccoli florets, broken into small pieces
¼	cup sliced black olives
1	Plum tomato, thinly sliced crosswise

Place pizza crust on large baking sheet. Spread pesto to within 1-inch of edge. Sprinkle with cheese. Sprinkle broccoli and olives over the cheese. Arrange tomato slices in a circle around outer edge of pizza.

Place baking sheet on lower rack in oven and bake 12 to 15 minutes, or until heated through and cheese has melted. Makes 6 servings.

Stove Top

Use your families favorite brand of salsa for this recipe. The process cheese spread to use is Velveeta® or American cheese.

Beef & Cheese Macaroni

1	pound lean ground beef
2	cups chunky salsa
2	cups uncooked elbow macaroni
8	ounces process cheese spread

Brown meat in a large skillet; drain.

Add salsa and 1¾ *cups water*. Bring to a boil and then add macaroni. Reduce heat to a simmer, cover and cook 8 minutes or until pasta is just tender.

While pasta is cooking, cut cheese into small cubes. Add to skillet and cook, stirring frequently, until melted. Makes 6 servings.

Slow Cooker

Beef & Salsa Dip

1	pound lean ground beef
16	ounces process cheese spread, cubed
1	(15-oz) can creamed corn
1½	cups salsa

Brown ground beef; drain and add to slow cooker. Add cheese along with remaining ingredients. Cook on High 1 to 1½ hours or until cheese is melted and mixture is hot. Turn heat to Low, until ready to serve, stirring occasionally. Serve with chips. Makes 5½ cups.

Chili con Queso

1	pound lean ground beef
1	cup chopped onion
1	(4-oz) can chopped green chilies
1	cup chunky salsa
2	pounds process cheese spread, cubed

In medium skillet, brown ground beef and onion; drain. Place in slow cooker. Add remaining ingredients. Cover and cook on Low 2 to 3 hours, stirring to blend when cheese is partially melted. Makes about 6 cups.

Stove Top
Slow Cooker

This is so good I doubt you'll have leftovers, but if you do, serve over baked potatoes for a quick and easy lunch or dinner.

Stove Top
Slow Cooker

Serve with chips or toasted bread cubes.

Rely on your slow cooker for meals on those extra busy days.

Easy Tender Ribs

1   rack baby back ribs
     Salt and pepper
     Choice of barbecue sauce

Cut ribs in half crosswise. Sprinkle both sides with salt and pepper and place in slow cooker, meaty-side up. Add *½ cup water*. Cover and cook on Low 6 to 7 hours or until tender. Cut into individual ribs and serve with your favorite sauce. Makes 2 to 3 servings.

This recipe is very similar to the following recipe, except the sauce is added at the table.

Barbecue Ribs

1½   **racks baby back ribs, about 20 ribs**
     Choice of barbecue sauce

Wash and trim ribs of excess fat. Cut into 2-rib sections. Brush both sides of ribs with barbecue sauce. Place as many ribs, meaty-side out, as you can around the pot. Place remaining ribs on the bottom, meaty-side up. Cover and cook on Low 6 to 7 hours or until tender. Makes 4 to 5 servings.

I don't know anyone who will turn down ribs. They are moist, tender and delicious cooked in a slow cooker. You may want to brush additional sauce on the ribs just before serving or pass extra sauce at the table

Remember

Slow cookers can vary quite a bit as far as their cooking times. We have found that the newer ones cook at a higher temperature and faster than the older ones. Each time you make a new recipe, note the cooking time and write it down.

Getting Organized

**How do you meet the daily challenge of getting dinner on the table?
You get organized.**

1. Plan a weekly menu - this isn't always fun, but believe me, it will save you time and money in the long run.

2. Make a shopping list. Check your pantry first, then make a list of everything you will need for the next week's menus.

3. Plan on cooking a roast, small turkey or ham for Sunday's dinner. Then plan that week's menus around the leftovers.

4. If you're making a casserole or spaghetti sauce, make twice as much and freeze one.

5. To save even more money, plan your meals using the supermarkets' weekly specials.

Best-Ever Chili

1½	pounds lean ground beef
1½	cups coarsely chopped onion
1	to 2 tablespoons chili powder (or to taste)
1	(19-oz) can dark red kidney beans, drained, rinsed
1	(28-oz) jar pasta sauce (I used Tomato & Basil)

In a large skillet, brown ground beef, onion and chili powder; drain off fat. Spoon into slow cooker and add beans and pasta sauce, stirring to mix.

Cover and cook on LOW about 4 hours or on HIGH for 2 hours. Makes 6 cups.

Stove Top
Slow Cooker

This is very good, easy to make and smells wonderful cooking in the slow cooker.

The most time consuming part of this recipe is cooking the pasta. The rest is easy.

Ham & Pasta Parmesan

12	ounces linguine
¼	cup butter
½	cup heavy cream
⅓	cup sliced green onions, green part
1	cup diced ham
½	cup grated Parmesan cheese

Cook pasta according to package directions. Rinse and drain. Add pasta and butter to sprayed slow cooker and toss to melt the butter. Add remaining ingredients along with ½ *cup water.*

Cover. Cook on LOW until heated through but probably no longer than an hour, or it will tend to get a little dry. If this should happen, stir in additional cream. Makes 6 servings.

By cooking the final stages of this recipe in a slow cooker, you can rest assured the eggs will be cooked through.

Carbonara

12	ounces spaghetti
12	slices bacon, cooked, crumbled
½	cup butter
3	large eggs, lightly beaten
¾	cup grated Parmesan cheese

Cook pasta according to package directions. Rinse and drain, but save ½ cup of the liquid. Place pasta in a sprayed slow cooker.

Add remaining ingredients and mix well. If mixture seems a little dry, add some of the reserved pasta water. Cover. Cook on LOW to finish cooking the eggs and to keep the pasta hot, about 1 hour. Makes 6 servings.

Macaroni & Cheese

Stove Top
Slow Cooker

2½	cups elbow macaroni
2	large eggs, lightly beaten
1	tablespoon prepared mustard
⅛	teaspoon pepper
1	cup heavy cream
4	cups (16-oz) Cheddar cheese, shredded

Prepare and keep hot in your slow cooker.

Cook pasta according to package directions. Rinse and drain. Add to sprayed slow cooker.

Combine eggs, mustard, pepper, cream, and *1 cup water*. Add to pasta and mix well. Add cheese. Cover. Cook on HIGH 2 hours or until heated through and the cheese has melted. Stir after 1 to 1½ hours, stirring the outer edges into the center.

Cook just until hot in the center and the mixture is nice and creamy. After that, the cheese might separate somewhat. It will still taste good, but it may not look as good. Makes 10 servings.

Who would have thought?

Entertaining and short on oven space or time?

Make mashed potatoes ahead of time and keep hot in your slow cooker. Set slow cooker on LOW, top with a tablespoon or two of butter and cover until ready to serve.

When I know I'm going to have a busy day or I'm going to be gone all day, I love to use my slow cooker. Plan ahead and you can have a meal on the table in minutes.

Family Pot Roast

1	(5 to 6-lb) rump roast
12	small new potatoes
6	carrots
1	large onion
1	teaspoon seasoning salt

Place half the potatoes in slow cooker. Cut carrots into 2-inch pieces and onion into wedges; place half over potatoes. Add roast and arrange remaining vegetables around meat. Add *1 cup water.* Sprinkle with salt. Cover and cook on Low 10 to 12 hours. If you happen to be at home, halfway through cooking time, push the vegetables down into the liquid. Makes 6 to 8 servings.

Stove Top Slow Cooker

This dish smells so good when you come home from a soccer game or a day of winter errands.

Chili Beef Dish

1½	pounds lean ground beef
1½	cups chopped onion
3	large Plum tomatoes, diced
2	(15-oz) cans chili with beans

In a large skillet, brown ground beef and onion. Place in slow cooker. Add tomatoes and chili. Cover and cook on Low 4 to 5 hours. Makes about 8 servings.

One hour on High
equals
Two hours on Low

Ground Beef & Cheese Soup

1	pound ground beef
⅔	cup chopped onion
2	cups cubed potatoes
1	cup peas
1	cup corn
16	ounces process cheese spread, cubed

Brown ground beef and onion in a large skillet; drain. Place in slow cooker. Add potatoes and *2 cups water*. Cook on Low 8 to 10 hours.

Add corn and peas and cook about 20 minutes, or until heated through.

Add cheese cubes, and cook 5 to 10 minutes or until melted. Stir to blend. Makes 7 cups.

Chunky Applesauce

5	large Golden Delicious apples
5	large Rome apples
¾	cup sugar
½	teaspoon cinnamon
¼	teaspoon ground ginger
5	large strips of fresh orange peel

Peel, slice and core apples. Cut into ¼ to ½-inch slices. You should have about 12 cups. Place in slow cooker along with remaining ingredients and *¼ cup water*. Cover and cook on Low 8 to 10 hours, stirring about every two hours. The apples should be soft, but not mushy. Remove orange peel and discard. Makes 5 to 6 cups.

Stove Top Slow Cooker

Everyone in my family was amazed by this delicious soup. They didn't think they liked process cheese, but they loved this recipe.

Note: The soup may be quite thick when reheated. You can thin with milk or broth.
Potatoes take a long time to cook in a slow cooker. To shorten the cooking time, you can partially cook the potatoes in the microwave before adding to the slow cooker.

Serve with Garlic
Mashed Potatoes,
sauteed yellow
squash and a Caesar
Salad and you have
an easy and delicious
company meal.

This is a wonderful
recipe, convenient
and almost fail-proof.

Florentine Salmon

4	(6-oz) salmon fillets
2	tablespoons butter
¾	cup sliced small mushrooms
⅓	cup sliced green onions
½	bunch fresh spinach
⅓	cup dry white wine

In a large skillet, quickly sauté mushrooms and onions in the butter. Add spinach and toss to mix. Cook mixture until spinach is just slightly wilted.

Cut a long slit in top of each fillet and spread slightly. Fill pockets with spinach mixture. Place in a sprayed slow cooker and add the wine. Cover and cook on Low 1½ to 2 hours or until salmon tests done. Makes 4 servings.

Chicken Fettuccine

½	cup butter, plus 3 tablespoons
1	cup heavy whipping cream
1	cup freshly grated Parmesan cheese
¼	teaspoon pepper
3	chicken breast halves, skinned, boned
8	ounces fettuccine

Place the ½ cup butter, cream, Parmesan and pepper in slow cooker. Cover and cook on Low about 45 minutes or until ingredients are melted; stir to mix.

Meanwhile, cut chicken into bite-size pieces and cook in remaining butter in large skillet. Drain and set aside.

Cook pasta according to directions on package. Drain and add to slow cooker along with the chicken. Serve immediately, or cover and keep hot until ready to serve. Makes 4 servings.

Salads, Dressings, Sauces

Brie Salad

8	cups mixed greens
2	tablespoons sliced almonds
⅓	cup vinaigrette dressing
4	(1-inch) wedges Brie cheese

Combine greens and almonds in a large mixing bowl. Toss with just enough dressing to lightly coat.

Place salad on serving plates. Place Brie on a baking sheet and bake about 1 minute or until warm, but not runny. Top each salad with a cheese wedge. Makes 4 servings.

Oven 350°F

Other types of cheese can be substituted for the Brie.

Romaine Artichoke Salad

8	cups romaine
1	(6.5-oz) jar marinated artichoke hearts, drained
6	tablespoons oil
2	tablespoons garlic red wine vinegar
¼	cup grated Parmesan cheese, divided
8	cherry tomatoes, halved

Place romaine in a large salad bowl. Cut artichokes into smaller pieces and add to bowl.

Combine oil, vinegar and 2 tablespoons of the Parmesan. Toss salad with just enough dressing to lightly coat. Serve on salad plates. Sprinkle with remaining Parmesan and garnish with tomatoes. Makes 8 servings.

A perfect salad with almost any meal.

Salad Suggestions

Do you ever get tired of making the same old salad? These suggestions should give you a good start and provide an assortment of delicious salads. Omit or add ingredients according to what you and your family enjoy. Use your favorite prepared or purchased dressing.

10 ounces spinach
½ cup shredded purple cabbage
⅓ cup raisins
¼ cup sliced almonds

10 ounces spinach
1 red onion, thinly sliced
1 cup fresh strawberries, sliced
⅓ cup pecan halves

1 large head romaine
2 kiwis, peeled, sliced
1 avocado, cubed
⅓ cup pecan halves

6 cups assorted greens
4 ounces mushrooms, sliced
8 slices bacon, cook, crumbled
4 green onions, sliced

10 ounces spinach
2 small fresh nectarines
2 fresh plums, sliced
½ English cucumber, chopped

1 large head romaine
1 cup cooked, cubed chicken
⅓ cup dried cranberries
⅓ cup sliced almonds

6 cups assorted greens
4 ounces Swiss cheese, cubed
1 cup red seedless grapes, halved
8 slices bacon, cooked, crumbled

1 large head romaine
½ red pepper, diced
Mushrooms, sliced
Red onion, thinly sliced

1 large head romaine
8 slices bacon, cooked, crumbled
2 ounces feta or blue cheese
⅓ cup coarsely chopped walnuts
1 apple, thinly sliced or cubed

6 cups assorted greens
Carrot strips
Cherry tomatoes, halved
Red onion, thinly sliced
Black olives

Salads with fruit usually taste better if you use a sweet-sour or poppy seed type of dressing. Salads with a lot of veggies generally taste better with a vinaigrette, Italian or Ranch dressing.

Apple–Pear Green Salad

12	cups mixed salad greens (use mostly romaine)
1	medium red skin apple, cubed
1	medium green pear, cubed
½	cup dried cranberries
¾	cup whole cashews
¾	cup Poppy Seed dressing (approximately)

In a large mixing bowl, combine the first 5 ingredients. Add just enough dressing to lightly coat, stirring until salad is well mixed. Makes 6 to 8 servings.

If time allows make the Poppy Seed Dressing, page 239. It will make all the difference in a good salad and a great salad.

Caesar Salad

2	bunches romaine (about 8 cups)
	Croutons
½	cup Caesar Salad Dressing, page 240
3	tablespoons grated Parmesan cheese

Tear romaine into bite-size pieces. Place romaine and croutons in a large salad bowl. Toss with just enough dressing to lightly coat. Spoon onto salad plates and sprinkle with cheese. Makes 6 servings.

I made this salad for my daughter's birthday and there wasn't even a lettuce leaf left in the bowl. For a main dish salad, add some cooked chicken and serve with your favorite homemade or purchased breads or muffins.

Caesar Salad Hint

Although not exactly traditional, you can enhance these wonderful salads by adding your choice of the following items: chicken, turkey, salmon, shrimp, fried oysters, bacon, sun-dried tomatoes, or penne pasta.

Sweet–Sour Spinach Salad

1	bunch fresh spinach or about 1 bag
1	tablespoon white vinegar
1	tablespoon sugar
¼	cup mayonnaise
1	very small red onion, thinly sliced, separated into rings
8	slices bacon, cooked, crumbled

Wash spinach thoroughly and dry. Remove long stems and tear into bite-size pieces; chill.

Combine vinegar, sugar, and mayonnaise; chill.

When ready to serve, combine spinach, onion, and bacon. Toss with just enough dressing to lightly coat. Serve immediately; greens have a tendency to get limp if allowed to set very long. Makes 3 to 4 servings.

Crisp Green Salad

4	cups assorted salad greens
1	cup cherry tomatoes
1	cup cauliflower florets
½	green pepper, sliced
½	small cucumber, sliced
	Choice of dressing

Combine first 5 ingredients in salad bowl. Toss with your favorite salad dressing. Makes 6 servings.

Raspberry-Spinach Salad

5	cups fresh spinach
1	cup fresh raspberries
½	cup chopped macadamia nuts
	Raspberry Vinaigrette, page 242

Combine ingredients in salad bowl and toss with just enough dressing to lightly coat. Makes 4 servings.

The dressing can be made ahead and chilled.

Summer Fruit Salad

6	cups mixed greens
1	cup small green grapes
1	(11-oz)) can Mandarin oranges, drained
¼	cup chopped red onion
⅓	cup sliced almonds
	Choice of dressing

Place first 5 ingredients in a large mixing bowl. Toss with just enough dressing to lightly coat. Makes 4 to 6 servings.

Either the Poppy Seed or the Honey Mustard Dressing would be good on this salad.

Pineapple-Strawberry Salad

1	cup fresh pineapple chunks
1	pint strawberries
	Lettuce leaves
2	tablespoons oil
2	tablespoons lime juice
1	tablespoon honey

Combine pineapple and strawberries; place on lettuce leaves on salad plates. Combine remaining ingredients and drizzle over fruit. Makes 4 servings.

With fresh fruits on hand, this salad takes just minutes to prepare.

Cobb Salad

8	cups shredded lettuce
2	cups cubed, cooked chicken
1	medium tomato, chopped
2	hardboiled eggs, chopped
8	slices bacon, cooked, crumbled
½	cup Ranch dressing

Arrange lettuce on four plates. Divide rows of chicken, tomato, and egg on plates. Sprinkle with bacon and drizzle with dressing. Makes about 6 servings.

Variation:
If desired, you can place all of the ingredients in a large salad bowl and toss to coat.

Waldorf Chicken Salad

3	cups cubed, cooked chicken
⅓	cup chopped celery
¾	cup chopped jicama
⅓	cup chopped walnuts
½	cup mayonnaise

Combine first 4 ingredients with just enough mayonnaise to moisten. Cover and chill before serving. Makes about 6 servings.

Chill

Jicama is a very good substitute for the apples tradition-ally found in Waldorf salads.

Company Spinach Salad

8	cups fresh spinach
½	cup toasted pecan halves
¾	cup strawberries, sliced
½	cup Poppy Seed Dressing, page 239

Combine first 3 ingredients in a large salad bowl. Toss with just enough dressing to lightly coat.

Variation: Substitute ¼ cup pomegranate seeds for the strawberries. Makes 6 servings.

A nice touch of color for a special company dinner.

Easy Club Salad

	Lettuce leaves
3	slices cooked chicken
3	slices tomato
3	slices bacon, cooked, crumbled
2	tablespoons Thousand Island Dressing, page 242

Arrange lettuce leaves on salad plate. Top with chicken, tomato slices, then bacon. Drizzle with dressing. Makes 1 serving.

Tastes like a club sandwich minus the bread.

Wilted Lettuce

If you have some lettuce that is a little soft and droopy, but not brown, it may be dehydrated. You can, sometimes, revive it by sprinkling lightly with water and chilling.

Variation:
Substitute 1 cup
thick and chunky
salsa for the season-
ing mix.

Taco Salad

1	pound lean ground beef
1	(1¼-oz) package Taco seasoning mix
	Shredded lettuce
	Shredded Cheddar cheese
	Chopped tomatoes
	Salsa (or Thousand Island Dressing)

Brown ground beef; drain. Add seasoning mix and amount of water called for on package. Bring to a boil; reduce heat and simmer uncovered, 15 to 20 minutes, stirring occasionally until liquid is absorbed.

Place shredded lettuce in salad bowl; top with ground beef, cheese, tomatoes, and salsa. Toss lightly and serve. Makes 4 servings.

Serve on a bed of
lettuce as a salad or
on toasted bread
for a sandwich. To
make the salad go a
little farther, add 1 to
2 hardboiled eggs,
chopped.

Ham Salad

2	cups (8-oz) cooked ham, ground
1	teaspoon prepared mustard
3	tablespoons sweet pickle relish
½	cup diced Cheddar cheese
½	cup mayonnaise (approximately)

In a small mixing bowl, combine first 4 ingredients. Add enough of the mayonnaise to moisten. Makes about 2 cups.

Coconut Chicken Salad

4	cups diced cooked chicken
½	cup thinly sliced celery
½	cup flaked coconut
½	teaspoon curry, or to taste
1	cup mayonnaise

Combine first 3 ingredients in a mixing bowl.

Combine curry and mayonnaise. Add just enough mayonnaise to chicken to moisten. Chill until ready to serve. Makes 4 servings.

Chill

Variation:
Add ½ cup drained crushed pineapple.

Chicken Pecan Salad

2	cups cubed, cooked chicken
½	cup pecan halves, broken in half
⅓	cup chopped celery
½	cup mayonnaise

Combine ingredients, adding just enough mayonnaise to moisten. Cover and chill until ready to serve. Makes 2 large or 3 small servings.

Chill

This recipe works wonderfully as a salad, a sandwich, or to fill cream puffs, croissants, or cantaloupe halves.

Variation:
Add ⅓ cup dried cranberries.

Pasta Herb Chicken Salad

One of our local restaurants serves a delicious pasta salad with chicken. This recipe comes very close to the one they make.

1½	cups cubed, cooked chicken
2½	cups cooked rotini pasta
1	head lettuce, torn into bite-size pieces
¼	cup grated carrots
½	cup sliced almonds
	Bernstein's® Creamy Herb & Garlic Italian Dressing

Combine first 5 ingredients in a large mixing bowl. Toss with just enough dressing to lightly coat. Makes 4 to 6 servings.

Chill

Tuna–Pineapple Salad

The pineapple adds a nice touch to what is usually a pretty standard tuna salad.

2	(6-oz) cans tuna, drained
1	(8-oz) can crushed pineapple, drained
½	cup finely chopped celery
2	large hardboiled eggs, chopped
⅓	cup mayonnaise

Combine first 4 ingredients and toss with just enough mayonnaise to lightly coat. Cover and chill before serving. Makes 4 servings.

Chicken and Pasta Salad

Chicken, pasta, and greens combine to make a full-meal salad. Combine a 9 or 12-ounce package refrigerated cheese tortellini, cooked and chilled, with one bag assorted greens. Add about 2 to 3 cups cubed, cooked chicken, some croutons, and then toss with Caesar dressing. Sprinkle with shredded Parmesan cheese. Makes 4 to 6 servings.

Broccoli-Cranberry Pasta Salad

1	(12-oz) package rotini
4	cups small broccoli florets
⅓	cup dried cranberries
2	cups mayonnaise
⅔	cup sugar
⅓	cup white vinegar

Cook pasta according to directions on package. Rinse until cool and drain thoroughly. Place in a large mixing bowl and stir in the broccoli and cranberries.

Combine remaining ingredients and stir to dissolve the sugar. Add half the dressing to the pasta mixture. Cover and chill at least 2 hours before serving.

When ready to serve, add additional dressing, if needed. Save remaining dressing for any leftover salad the next day. Makes 6 to 8 servings.

Note: The dressing may seem like a lot and it would be with just the broccoli, but the pasta quickly absorbs a lot of dressing.

Stove Top Chill

This salad has become another of my new favorite salads. If desired, omit the cranberries and add ½ cup of split cashews, just before serving.

Broccoli Pasta Salad

2	cups small shell macaroni, cooked, cooled
2½	cups fresh broccoli florets
1	cup cherry tomatoes, halved
½	cup (2-oz) Swiss cheese, cubed
½	cup Italian dressing

Combine ingredients in a large bowl using just enough dressing to lightly coat. Cover and chill. Makes 8 servings.

Stove Top Chill

Depending on how much dressing the pasta absorbs, you may have to add more just before serving.

This is a delicious combination. For a complete meal just add cooked chicken or shrimp. If desired, you may moisten with a little milk before serving.

This is always a great pot luck or buffet favorite.

Linda's Pesto Pasta Salad

3	cups penne
1	(9-oz) can artichokes hearts, diced
1	cup frozen peas, thawed
¾	cup pesto
¼	cup mayonnaise
½	to 1 cup shredded Parmesan cheese

Cook pasta according to directions on package. Rinse until cool and drain thoroughly. Place in a large mixing bowl and stir in remaining ingredients. Cover and chill at least 2 hours before serving. Makes 6 to 8 servings.

Chicken Pasta Salad

8	ounces rotini, cooked, drained and cooled
1½	cups cubed cooked chicken
½	cup frozen peas, thawed
1	cup (4-oz) Mozzarella cheese, diced
½	cup mayonnaise
½	cup Parmesan Ranch salad dressing

In large mixing bowl, combine first 4 ingredients. Combine mayonnaise and salad dressing. Add about half to the mixing bowl tossing to coat.

Cover and chill until ready to serve. A lot of the dressing will be absorbed into the salad. Add remaining dressing as needed. Makes 6 servings.

Family Coleslaw

4	cups shredded cabbage
½	cup raisins
½	cup mayonnaise
1	tablespoon milk
1	tablespoon sugar

Combine cabbage and raisins. In small mixing bowl, combine remaining ingredients and pour over cabbage; mix well. Cover and chill at least 30 minutes before serving. Makes 4 to 6 servings.

Chill

The dressing makes the salad, so choose a brand you really enjoy or better yet, make your own.

Waldorf Coleslaw

4	to 5 cups shredded cabbage
½	cup dried cranberries
⅓	cup chopped pecans
1	apple, cubed
⅔	cup mayonnaise
2	tablespoons sugar

Place the first 4 ingredients in large mixing bowl. Combine mayonnaise and sugar, blending thoroughly. Continue to stir until sugar is somewhat dissolved. If too thick, you can add about a tablespoon of milk, but you probably won't find this necessary.

Toss cole slaw with just enough mayonnaise to coat. Cover and chill at least 1 hour before serving. Makes about 6 servings.

Chill

This is at it's best served same day made.

Waldorf Salad

2	Golden Delicious apples, cubed
1	cup sliced celery
⅓	cup coarsely chopped walnuts
½	cup raisins
2	tablespoons lemon juice
¾	cup mayonnaise

Still a favorite salad with almost everyone. For a main course salad, add 2 cups cooked, cubed chicken.

Combine first 5 ingredients in mixing bowl. Add mayonnaise and gently toss to coat. Chill until ready to serve. Makes 4 servings.

Broccoli Bean Salad

4	cups broccoli florets
4	Plum tomatoes, chopped
1	(8¾-oz) can garbanzo beans, drained
1	small red onion, sliced
1	cup (4-oz) Monterey Jack cheese, cubed
¾	cup Italian style dressing

Take this salad along to a barbecue or summer potluck.

In a small mixing bowl, combine first 5 ingredients. Add just enough of the dressing to lightly coat. Makes about 2 cups.

Best Ever Broccoli Salad

1	large bunch broccoli (about 5 cups florets)
1	cup (4-oz) Monterey Jack cheese, cubed
½	cup sugar
1	cup mayonnaise
2	tablespoons white vinegar
8	slices bacon, cooked and crumbled

Place broccoli and cheese in a large bowl.

Combine sugar, mayonnaise, and vinegar, stirring until smooth. Pour over broccoli and mix well. Cover and chill about 2 hours before serving, stirring occasionally. When ready to serve, add bacon and toss. Makes 6 servings.

Chill

There are many variations of this colorful, and nutritious salad. Any of the following are delicious additions: sliced red onion, raisins, sunflower seeds, Cheddar cheese, sliced water chestnuts, almonds, dried cranberries, etc.

My Favorite Potato Salad

6	medium red potatoes
	Salt and pepper
2	tablespoons chopped green onion
3	hardboiled eggs, chopped
¼	cup finely chopped celery
1¼	cups mayonnaise (approximately)

Cook potatoes in boiling water just until tender. Cool slightly; peel. While still warm, dice potatoes and sprinkle with salt and pepper. Add remaining ingredients; toss gently to mix. Cover and chill several hours or overnight. Makes 8 servings.

Stove top Chill

For additional color, add 2 tablespoons finely chopped pimento. If desired, decorate top of salad with egg slices and tomato wedges; sprinkle with cracked pepper.

Garden Tomato Salad

Sliced red and/or yellow tomatoes
Thinly sliced red onion
Olive oil
Salt and pepper

Arrange tomatoes on a serving platter. Arrange onion over top. Drizzle with a small amount of oil. Sprinkle lightly with salt and pepper.

Variation: for a little zip to this recipe add a drizzle of Balsamic vinegar.

Save this salad for when home-grown tomatoes are available either from your garden or your local farmer's market.

Asparagus Salad

Stove Top Chill

For the best results, use when fresh asparagus is in season.

1	**pound fresh asparagus, trimmed**
4	**romaine or other lettuce leaves**
2	**medium tomatoes, sliced**
	Italian dressing

In a large skillet, cook asparagus in about ½-inch of water, until just crisp-tender. Rinse and chill until ready to serve.

Place a lettuce leaf on each salad plate. Place tomato slices on top of lettuce. Top with the asparagus and drizzle lightly with dressing. Makes 4 servings.

To Gel or Not to Gel

Look in most cookbooks in your bookstore and you won't find a "Jello" salad recipe on any of the pages. But look in a Junior League, Church or Club cookbook and you will find page after page of contributors' favorite gelatin recipes. Let's face it, they are colorful, versatile, refreshing, delicious and something most kids will eat. So forget about what some cookbook authors say and enjoy your gelatin salads. Try some of the recipes on these pages and you might just add a new one to your list of family favorites.

Peachy Fruit Salad

1	**(6-oz) box strawberry gelatin**
4	**cups boiling water, divided**
1	**cup thinly sliced peaches**
½	**cup thinly sliced bananas**
½	**cup thinly sliced strawberries**

Combine gelatin and 2 cups water. Stir until dissolved. Add remaining 2 cups water. Chill until consistency of unbeaten egg white. Gently fold in fruit. Pour into 13x9-inch glass dish; chill until firm. Makes 8 servings.

Chill

You shouldn't have a problem getting your children to eat this delicious "fruity" salad.

Strawberry Nut Salad

1	**(3-oz) box strawberry gelatin**
½	**cup boiling water**
1	**(10-oz) package frozen strawberries, thawed**
1	**(13-oz) can crushed pineapple (and juice)**
2	**medium bananas, mashed**
½	**cup chopped walnuts**

Combine gelatin and water, stirring to dissolve. Add remaining ingredients. Pour into a 5 cup mold or 11x7-inch glass dish. Chill until set. Makes 8 servings.

Chill

A simple version of a very old recipe. Don't plan on having any left-overs.

If desired, garnish
each serving with a
combination of fresh
fruits such as rasp-
berries, blueberries
and/or peaches and
garnish with a mint
leaf.

Orange Sherbet Salad

1	(6-oz) box orange gelatin
1	pint orange sherbet, softened
2	(11-oz) cans Mandarin oranges, save juice
1	(8-oz) can crushed pineapple, save juice
1	cup whipping cream, whipped

Pour juice in measuring cup; add water to make 2 cups. Heat to boiling in saucepan. Remove from heat; add gelatin and stir until dissolved. Add sherbet; stir until melted. Chill until just slightly thickened.

Add Mandarin oranges and pineapple; fold in whipped cream. Pour into a ring mold or 11x7-inch glass dish. Chill until set. Makes 8 servings.

Chill

The celery adds a
nice crunch, but can
be omitted.

Lemon Fruit Salad

1	(6-oz) box lemon gelatin
1	cup boiling water
2	cups lemon-lime soda
½	cup raspberries
½	cup sliced strawberries
⅓	cup thinly sliced celery

Thoroughly dissolve gelatin in boiling water. Add soda. Chill until consistency of unbeaten egg white.

Fold in fruit and celery. Pour into an 11x7-inch glass baking dish. Chill until set. Makes 8 servings.

Berry-Berry Fruit Salad

Chill

1 (6-oz) box strawberry gelatin
1 cup sliced strawberries
1 cup raspberries

Prepare gelatin as directed on package. Pour into an 11x7-inch baking dish. Chill until consistency of egg whites.

Gently fold in berries. At this point you can keep mixture in dish or pour into a mold. Chill until set.

Serve as a salad or a light dessert. Only 85 calories per serving if using a sugar free gelatin.

Strawberries & Cream Salad

Chill

1 (3-oz) box strawberry gelatin
1 cup boiling water
1 cup sour cream, room temperature
1 (10-oz) package frozen strawberries, thawed

Combine gelatin and water; stir to dissolve. Stir in sour cream until blended. Add strawberries. Pour into serving dish or mold and chill until set. Makes 6 servings.

Make sure your sour cream is at room temperature. If you have a little difficulty blending in the sour cream, use a rotary beater or a mixer at low speed.

Watching your calories or sugar?

Here's a satisfying dessert or treat:

First make a sugar free gelatin, containing chopped strawberries and blueberries. Chill this in an 11x7-inch baking dish. When firm, slice into bite-size cubes.

In parfait or wine glasses, layer cubed gelatin, sugar free whipped topping and a few chopped nuts. Make 2 layers of each. Enjoy!

Honeydew Slices

Honeydew melon, chilled, sliced crosswise into 1½-inch slices, seeds removed
Cantaloupe balls
Watermelon balls
Fresh mint leaves (optional)

Place a honeydew slice on individual salad plates. Fill each with cantaloupe and watermelon balls. Garnish with mint leaves.

If honeydew melon is too large to make attractive slices, you could use a cantaloupe and make honeydew melon balls. Tuck in a few blueberries or sliced strawberries if you have them.

Variation:
Sour cream can be substituted for the whipped topping, if desired.

All Seasons Fruit Salad

6	canned pear halves, chilled
3	medium bananas, sliced
2	small apples, cubed
2	(11-oz) cans Mandarin oranges, chilled
1 ½	cups sliced strawberries
1	(4-oz) container frozen whipped topping, thawed

When ready to serve, drain fruit. Slice pears. Combine with remaining ingredients and toss gently to coat. Makes 6 servings.

Pudding & Fruit Salad

1   (3.4-oz) box instant vanilla pudding mix
2   cups milk
1   (4-oz) container frozen whipped topping, thawed
1   (11-oz) can Mandarin oranges, drained
1   (16-oz) can fruit cocktail, drained
3   bananas, sliced

Prepare pudding mix with milk as directed on package. Stir in whipped topping. Add the remaining ingredients. Pour into a 11x7-inch glass dish. Cover and freeze. Remove from freezer 1 hour before serving. Or, instead of freezing, place in refrigerator and chill at least 2 hours before serving. Makes about 8 servings.

This fruit salad is a hit with children (adults too). If you choose not to freeze the salad (my favorite), it is best served same day made.

Pistachio Fruit Salad

1   (12-oz) container frozen whipped topping, thawed
1   (3.4-oz) box pistachio instant pudding mix
1   (11-oz) can Mandarin oranges, save 3 table-spoons juice
1   (17-oz) can chunky mixed fruits, drained
2   cups miniature marshmallows

In large bowl, combine whipped topping and pudding mix with the reserved juice. Gently fold in remaining ingredients. Cover and chill. Makes 6 to 8 servings.

Chill

This delicious recipe has stood the test of time. It is the perfect accompaniment to a summer's barbecue.

Sweet Onion Dressing

½   cup olive oil
¼   cup cider vinegar
¼   cup finely chopped onion
½   teaspoon prepared mustard
½   teaspoon salt
1   tablespoon sugar

This dressing is especially good on spinach salads and has an added bonus of keeping several days in the refrigerator.

Combine ingredients, mixing well to blend. Chill until ready to use. Makes 1 cup.

Creamy Mustard Dressing

¼   cup Dijon mustard
¾   teaspoon dried dill weed
¼   cup tarragon wine vinegar
1   cup oil
1   tablespoon Half & Half
1   tablespoon grated Parmesan cheese

This is a wonderful dressing for anyone who is on a low-carb diet. Just one carbohydrage gram per 2 tablespoons of dressing.

Combine mustard, dill weed and vinegar. Gradually add oil, whisking after each addition until blended. Stir in Half & Half and Parmesan. Makes 1½ cups.

Honey Mustard Dressing

1   cup mayonnaise
1   tablespoon sugar
1   tablespoon prepared mustard
1   tablespoon honey
1   teaspoon fresh lemon juice
     Dash of salt and pepper or to taste

Combine all ingredients and beat with a whisk until well mixed. Cover and chill until ready to serve. Makes 1 cup.

Poppy Seed Dressing

1   tablespoon finely chopped onion
6   tablespoons sugar
½   teaspoon dry mustard
3   tablespoons white vinegar
½   cup vegetable oil
½   teaspoon poppy seeds

Combine ingredients in a small bowl or jar and mix thoroughly. Cover and chill at least one hour to blend flavors. Let stand at room temperature 30 minutes before using. Makes 1 cup.

Chill

This dressing is very good on a tossed salad or a salad with pasta, chicken, lettuce and artichoke hearts. Dressing can be thinned with 1 to 2 teaspoons of milk, if necessary.

Chill

This popular recipe seems to be a hit with children as well as adults. The flavor is wonderful teamed with a spinach or romaine salad combined with some fruit, toasted nuts and pomegranate seeds.

Caesar Salad Dressing

Chill

This is my favorite Caesar salad dressing. You can make it several hours ahead. If desired, add anchovies to taste or toss the salad with anchovies.

2	large garlic cloves
1	tablespoon stone ground or Dijon mustard
1	teaspoon Worcestershire sauce
¼	cup fresh lemon juice
½	cup olive oil
½	cup freshly grated Parmesan cheese

Combine first 4 ingredients in a blender or small food processor and mix until smooth. Slowly add olive oil until blended. Add cheese and blend 2 to 3 seconds. Chill, covered, at least two hours to blend flavors. Makes 1¼ cups.

Creamy Caesar Dressing

Chill

Note: If you are in a hurry, use the minced garlic that comes in a jar.
½ teaspoon = 1 clove

1	medium garlic clove
¼	cup fresh lemon juice
1	tablespoon Dijon mustard
1	teaspoon Worcestershire sauce
½	cup freshly grated Parmesan cheese
1	cup mayonnaise

Combine first 4 ingredients in a blender or small food processor and process until mixed. (You can do this by hand if you mince the garlic first.) Add cheese and mayonnaise and process just until blended. Cover and chill at least one hour to allow flavors to blend. Makes about 1½ cups.

Dijon Vinaigrette

1¼	cups vegetable oil
⅓	cup Dijon mustard
⅓	cup garlic red wine vinegar
¼	teaspoon freshly ground black pepper

Place ingredients in a 2 cup jar or plastic container. Cover tightly and shake until blended. Will keep about one week. Makes about 1¾ cups.

This dressing is convenient to make ahead and chill.

Creamy Italian Dressing

¾	cup sour cream
⅓	cup mayonnaise
¼	cup milk
1	(.6-oz) package Italian dressing mix
2	tablespoons sugar
⅛	teaspoon salt (optional)

Combine ingredients until well mixed. Chill to blend flavors. Serve over salads or use as a dip with fresh vegetables. Makes about 1¼ cups.

Chill

The Italian dressing mix adds a nice touch to this creamy dressing.

Raspberry Vinaigrette

2	tablespoons sugar
¼	teaspoon salt
1	teaspoon Dijon mustard
3	tablespoons raspberry wine vinegar
⅓	cup olive oil

Combine all ingredients and mix thoroughly. Makes ½ cup.

Chill

A sweet-tart type of dressing. Can be made in just minutes and chilled until ready to use.

Thousand Island Dressing

½	cup mayonnaise
¼	cup whipping cream
2	tablespoons finely chopped pimiento
¼	cup chopped sweet pickles or pickle relish
1	tablespoon finely chopped onion
⅓	cup chili sauce

Combine ingredients and chill to blend flavors. Makes about ¾ cup.

Chill

Do try this recipe. It is so much better than any purchased dressing I have tried.

Red Wine Garlic Dressing

¼	cup sugar
1	garlic clove, thinly sliced
⅓	cup red wine vinegar
⅓	cup olive or vegetable oil

Combine ingredients and chill at least two hours to blend flavors. Remove garlic slices before tossing dressing with the salad. Makes about ¾ cup.

Chill

A sweet-sour type dressing that makes a delicious salad mixed with Romaine, red onion, mandarin oranges and toasted walnuts or pecans. This is the dressing I use most often for company. The Poppy Seed Dressing is a close second.

Chicken Salad Dressing

⅔ cup mayonnaise
⅓ cup sour cream
1 teaspoon lemon juice
½ teaspoon salt
¼ teaspoon pepper

Combine ingredients and mix well. Makes 1 cup.

This makes a wonderful dressing for almost any chunky style chicken salad.

French Dressing

⅓ cup vegetable oil
2 tablespoons red wine vinegar
2 tablespoons ketchup
¼ cup sugar
¼ teaspoon salt

Combine ingredients in a jar or small container with a tight fitting lid. Shake well to blend and dissolve sugar. Chill until ready to serve. Makes about ¾ cup.

Chill

This dressing is good on almost any green salad.

Mild Roquefort Dressing

Combine equal amounts of purchased Roquefort dressing with sour cream. Cover and chill until ready to use.

Family Favorite Barbecue Sauce

½ cup firmly packed brown sugar
1 cup ketchup
2 tablespoons Worcestershire sauce
1 tablespoon prepared mustard
¼ cup fresh lemon juice

Combine ingredients and let stand at least an hour to blend flavors. Serve at room temperature. Makes 1¾ cup.

Note: If making the recipe ahead, cover and store in the refrigerator.

Tartar Sauce

¾ cup mayonnaise
1 teaspoon finely chopped or grated onion
1 tablespoon finely chopped fresh parsley
1 tablespoon finely chopped sweet pickle

Combine ingredients; cover and chill at least 1 hour to blend flavors. Makes 1 cup.

Chill

Some people like tartar sauce with their French Fries. Personally, I think I'll stick with ketchup.

Snappy Horseradish Sauce

½   cup sour cream
¼   cup mayonnaise
1½ teaspoons prepared horseradish
¼   teaspoon onion salt
¼   teaspoon garlic salt

Combine ingredients and mix thoroughly. Cover and chill at least 1 hour to blend flavors. Makes ¾ cup.

Chill

For that special dinner, fill large mushroom caps with sauce; garnish with finely chopped chives or green onions and bake at 325° for 10 to 15 minutes. Serve on dinner plate with prime rib, roast beef, etc.

Orange Butter

½   cup butter, softened
1   tablespoon fresh orange zest

Beat ingredients until well blended.

Serve on French toast, pancakes, muffins or cornbread.

Mock Hollandaise Sauce

½   cup sour cream
½   cup mayonnaise
2   teaspoons fresh lemon juice
1   teaspoon prepared mustard

In a small saucepan, combine all the ingredients and cook over very low heat until heated through. Makes 1 cup.

Stove Top

So easy. Serve warm over cooked aparagus, broccoli, or green beans. Can be made ahead and reheated.

Orange Cream Cheese

1   (8-oz) package cream cheese, softened
¾   cup sifted powdered sugar
1   tablespoon frozen orange juice concentrate
1   tablespoon grated orange peel
1   tablespoon Grand Marnier Liqueur

In a mixer bowl, beat the cream cheese until smooth. Add remaining ingredients and mix until blended. Cover and chill. Makes 1¼ cups.

Chill

Serve with crackers, muffins, French toast or pancakes. Also good with fruit.

Stove Top

Yum! This is so good and also makes a wonderful fondue sauce.

Caramel Sauce

½	cup butter
¾	cup light corn syrup
1	(14-oz) can sweetened condensed milk
1½	cups packed brown sugar

Combine ingredients in a heavy medium saucepan. Cook over medium heat, stirring frequently, until sugar is dissolved. This should take about 8 to 10 minutes. Makes 3¼ cups.

Stove top

Keep this sauce on hand during the cold winter months when hot chocolate and snow are a match made in heaven. You can also use this recipe for delicious chocolate milk and of course as an ice cream topping. Tip: For best results use a good brand of chocolate chips. Do not use ultra-pasteurized cream or milk chocolate chips.

Chocolate Sauce Supreme

2	cups heavy cream
2	cups semisweet chocolate chips

Pour cream into a heavy medium saucepan. Over medium heat, bring to a boil. Remove from heat; add chocolate chips and stir quickly until chocolate is melted and sauce is smooth.

Pour into a container; cover and store in refrigerator. Makes 2½ cups. Mixture will thicken as it cools.

Hot Chocolate: Spoon about 4 tablespoons chocolate sauce (or to taste) in a 12-ounce mug. Fill with milk and microwave about 1½ minutes or until desired temperature.

Sweet and Sour Sauce

1	(6-oz) can pineapple juice
¼	cup apple cider vinegar
¼	cup finely packed brown sugar
1	tablespoon cornstarch

Combine ingredients in a small pan. Mix well to dissolve the sugar and cornstarch.

Cook over medium heat until mixture thickens, stirring frequently with a whisk. Makes ¾ cup.

Stove Top

Serve with chicken nuggets, chicken wings, egg rolls, etc.

Pizza Sauce

¼	teaspoon garlic powder
¼	teaspoon oregano
½	teaspoon basil
½	cup grated Parmesan cheese
1	(8-oz) can tomato sauce

In a small mixing bowl, combine all the ingredients and mix well. Makes about 1 cup.

If you run out of pizza sauce and don't want to make a special trip to the store, this makes a very good substitute.

Whole Berry Cranberry Sauce

Stove Top
Chill

Fresh cranberry sauce is so much better than any sauce purchased in a can. Do try it and I think you will agree with me. Leftover sauce can be frozen.Serve with turkey dinner or hot or cold turkey sandwiches.

1	pound fresh whole cranberries
2	cups sugar
½	cup apricot jam or preserves
¼	cup fresh lemon juice

Wash cranberries; discard the not so good ones. In a large saucepan, combine sugar and ¾ *cup water*. Bring to a boil and cook 3 to 4 minutes. Add cranberries and cook 6 to 8 minutes. Cranberries will burst, cause a popping sound and will become transparent.

Remove from heat and stir in apricot jam and lemon juice. Cover and chill before serving. Mixture will be a little thin but will thicken as it cools. Makes about 4 cups.

Easy Maple Syrup

Stove Top

This is so much better than the purchased imitation syrups on the market.

¼	cup light corn syrup
2	cups sugar
1	cup water
1	teaspoon maple flavoring

Combine corn syrup, sugar and water in a medium saucepan. Bring to a boil, stirring constantly. Cover and gently boil for 10 minutes. Remove from heat and allow to cool.

Add maple flavoring blending thoroughly. This is now ready to use or can be stored in the refrigerator. Makes about 1⅓ cups.

Safety First

Never use marinade in which raw meat, poultry or fish has been marinated. If you plan to use some of the marinade as a table sauce or to baste meat, remove the amount needed first, then marinate the meat in the remaining sauce. Double recipe if necessary.

Easy Beef Marinade

Use to marinate sirloin, chuck and flank steak.

Combine ingredients; pour over meat and marinate, in refrigerator, several hours or overnight, turning occasionally.

- ¼ **cup soy sauce**
- ¼ **cup oil**
- 2 **tablespoons fresh lemon juice**
- 1 **tablespoon sugar**
- ¼ **teaspoon garlic salt**
- ⅔ **teaspoon oregano**

Ginger Marinade

A good marinade for beef, pork or chicken.

Combine ingredients; pour over meat and marinate, in refrigerator, several hours or overnight, turning occasionally.

- ⅓ **cup soy sauce**
- ⅓ **cup packed brown sugar**
- 2 **tablespoons white vinegar**
- 1½ **tablespoons Worcestershire sauce**
- 1 **tablespoon olive oil**
- 3 **slices fresh ginger**

Herb Marinade

A good marinade for fish, chicken and meats.

Combine ingredients; pour over meat and marinate, in refrigerator, several hours or overnight, turning occasionally.

- ¼ **cup oil**
- 2 **tablespoons lemon juice**
- 1½ **tablespoons dry red wine**
- 1 **teaspoon dried thyme**
- 1 **medium garlic clove, minced**
- ¼ **teaspoon pepper**

If you don't have 4 cups turkey stock, add chicken broth or water to make up the difference. If gravy is too thin, stir in additional flour mixed with a small amount of water or stock. Add diced cooked turkey to leftover gravy. Reheat and serve over mashed potatoes, rice or noodles.

Tip: If gravy is too thick, stir in a little milk. If too thin, add a little flour mixed with a small amount of water.

Turkey Gravy

½ cup fat drippings
½ cup flour
4 cups turkey stock (from turkey or from cooking giblets)
Salt and pepper

Remove turkey from oven and pour meat juices into a large measuring cup. Fat will rise to the top. Pour off ½ cup fat into a medium saucepan. Discard remaining fat, but save the turkey stock.

Reheat the drippings over medium heat. Stir in flour and cook until lightly browned. Add 4 cups turkey stock. Cook over medium heat, stirring frequently, until thickened and smooth. Season with salt and pepper. Makes 4 cups.

Cream Gravy

4 tablespoons fat, from frying chicken (or other meats)
4 tablespoons flour
2 cups milk
Salt and pepper

Leave 4 tablespoons fat in pan along with the crusty bits that stick to the bottom. Heat until hot. Stir in flour and cook until brown and bubbly, stirring constantly.

Add milk and continue cooking, stirring frequently, until thickened and smooth, about 5 minutes. Add salt and pepper to taste. Makes 2 cups.

Vegetables

Hazelnut Asparagus

1	pound asparagus, trimmed
1	tablespoon butter
2	tablespoons chopped hazelnuts
¼	teaspoon dried basil
⅛	teaspoon ground pepper
2	tablespoons grated Parmesan cheese

Heat ¼ cup water in a medium skillet. Add asparagus and cook on medium-high heat 4 to 6 minutes or until just crisp-tender. Drain. Remove and set aside.

Add butter to skillet and sauté hazelnuts until lightly toasted. Return asparagus to skillet; season with basil and pepper and heat through. Place on serving plate and sprinkle with Parmesan.

Stove Top

My favorite asparagus recipe. Serve with Quiche Lorraine and a small Caesar salad.

Asparagus & Bacon

1	pound asparagus, using thin stalks
	Italian Dressing
4	slices bacon, cooked, crumbled

Wash asparagus; break off where it snaps easily. Place in skillet with hot water to cover. Cook over medium heat until crisp-tender; do not overcook. Remove immediately and drain thoroughly.

Toss with just enough dressing to lightly coat. Cover and chill (no longer than 2 to 3 hours) until ready to serve. Place on serving dish and sprinkle with bacon. Makes 4 servings.

Stove Top Chill

You will hear rave reviews every time you serve this dish and it couldn't be easier to make. Only three ingredients, and you could even omit the bacon and use just two ingredients. Serve as a side dish or as a salad.

A colorful green vegetable is the perfect side dish for your favorite family or company meal.

Steamed Green Beans

Desired amount of fresh green beans

Rinse beans and snap off ends. Cook in steamer rack over boiling water 10 to 15 minutes until just crisp-tender.
Or drop into a large pot of boiling water and cook 4 to 8 minutes or until just crisp-tender.

Asparagus with Butter Sauce

1	pound asparagus
1	cup chicken broth
3	tablespoons butter
3	tablespoons sliced almonds (optional)

Remove tough ends from asparagus; place in medium skillet. Add broth and bring to a boil. Reduce heat, cover and cook 6 to 8 minutes or until just crisp-tender.

Meanwhile, in a small skillet, lightly toast almonds in butter. Place asparagus in serving dish and cover with almond-butter sauce. Makes 4 servings.

Green Beans & Bacon

1	pound green beans, trimmed
1½	tablespoons butter
8	slices bacon, cooked, crumbled
	Salt and pepper

Cook beans in a large pot of boiling salted water until just crisp-tender, about 4 minutes or so. They will turn a bright green. Drain.

Heat butter in a large skillet; add beans and toss. Add bacon and heat through. Season with salt and pepper.

Snappy Company Beans

¼	cup butter
¼	cup finely chopped onion
2	teaspoons prepared mustard
1	teaspoon prepared horseradish
1	tablespoon packed brown sugar
1	pound fresh green beans

Combine the first 5 ingredients in a small saucepan. Heat just until butter is melted; mix thoroughly.

Spoon green beans into a 1½-quart casserole and spoon sauce over top. Bake 30 to 40 minutes or until heated through. Makes 4 servings.

Oven 350°F

Note: Two cans green beans, drained, can be substituted for the fresh. If increasing the recipe, make 3 times the recipe to serve 10 adults.

Variation:
Top with sliced tomatoes before baking.

Green Beans with Almonds

1	pound cooked green beans (or 1 can)
⅓	cup thinly sliced celery
¼	cup slivered almonds
2	tablespoons butter
	Salt and pepper

In medium skillet, sauté celery and almonds in butter until celery is tender and almonds are toasted. Add beans and heat through. Add salt and pepper to taste. Makes 4 servings.

Stove Top

Another easy green bean recipe.

Variation:
An addition of an
8-oz. can of crushed
pineapple is good. If
you have the time,
cook some chopped
onion and add to the
beans.

Just a touch of lemon
gives broccoli that
extra flavor it needs
to please most ap-
petites.

Note: Broccoli
spears can be cut so
they are 4 to 5 inches
in length or, for
company, I like to cut
them so the spears
are about 2½ inches
long.

Easy Baked Beans

2	(16-oz) cans pork and beans
½	cup firmly packed brown sugar
1	teaspoon dry mustard
½	cup ketchup
6	slices bacon, diced

Combine beans, brown sugar, mustard, and ketchup. Pour into a sprayed 1½-quart casserole. Top with bacon. Bake 1 to 1½ hours. Makes 6 servings.

Lemon Broccoli

¾	pound fresh broccoli spears
1½	tablespoons butter
1	tablespoon fresh lemon juice
¼	teaspoon salt
	Freshly ground black pepper

Place broccoli in a sprayed 11x7-inch baking dish. Add about ¼ cup water. Cover dish and microwave 4 to 6 minutes or until broccoli is bright green and just crisp-tender. Drain off water.

Combine remaining ingredients and microwave until butter is melted. Stir to blend ingredients; pour over broccoli. Makes 4 servings.

Broccoli with Bacon

4	slices bacon, cooked, crumbled
4	cups broccoli florets
3	tablespoons butter
¼	cup whole pecans
	Salt and pepper

Cook broccoli in a large saucepan of simmering water until just crisp-tender, about 3 to 4 minutes; drain

Meanwhile, heat butter in large skillet over medium heat. Add pecans and cook 1 minute. Add broccoli and bacon. Sprinkle with salt and pepper. Makes 4 servings.

Stove Top

A nice company dish. Serve with flank steak, baked potatoes and a salad.

Broccoli Meringue

5	cups broccoli florets
2	large egg whites, room temperature
¼	teaspoon salt
½	cup (2-oz) Edam, Cheddar, or Swiss cheese, shredded
½	cup mayonnaise

Microwave or steam broccoli; drain thoroughly. Place in a sprayed 8x8-inch baking dish.

Beat egg whites and salt until stiff peaks form. Fold in the cheese and mayonnaise. Spread evenly over broccoli. Broil 5 to 6 inches from heat 2 to 3 minutes or until golden brown. Makes 8 servings.

Steam
Broil

This is one recipe where the broccoli needs to be cooked beyond crisp-tender. It should be somewhat on the soft side.

Company Baked Carrots

Oven 350°F

My favorite carrot recipe. For such a simple recipe, it packs a lot of flavor.

1	pound carrots, sliced into ½-inch slices
3	tablespoons butter, sliced thin
1	tablespoon packed brown sugar
½	teaspoon salt
¼	teaspoon cracked pepper

Place carrots in a sprayed 1½-quart casserole. Distribute butter pieces over top. Sprinkle with brown sugar, salt, and cracked pepper. Cover and bake 45 to 60 minutes or until carrots are tender. Makes 4 servings.

Judy's Cauliflower Dish

Oven 350°F

Some of our best recipes come from our friends.

1	(20-oz) package frozen cauliflower, thawed
	Salt and pepper
1	cup mayonnaise
1	tablespoon prepared mustard
1	cup (4-oz) Cheddar cheese, shredded

Place cauliflower in a sprayed 8x8-inch baking dish. Bake 8 minutes. Sprinkle with salt and pepper.

Combine mayonnaise and mustard. Spread over cauliflower. Bake 8 minutes.

Sprinkle with cheese and bake 8 to 10 minutes or until cauliflower is tender. Makes 6 servings.

Cabbage Stir-Fry

Stove Top

2	tablespoons oil
6	cups cabbage (cut into 1½-inch slices)
	Salt and pepper

In a large skillet, heat oil over medium heat.

Add cabbage and ¼ *cup water*. Cook until just crisp-tender, about 8 to 10 minutes, stirring occasionally. Season with salt and pepper.

For color, add a small shredded carrot.

Brussels Sprouts Sauté

Stove Top

1	pound Brussels sprouts
¼	cup butter
½	teaspoon basil
	Salt and pepper to taste

Trim Brussels sprouts and remove outer leaves. Cut each, crosswise, into 3 or 4 slices.

Heat butter in medium skillet. Add Brussels sprouts and remaining ingredients and toss to coat. Cook 8 to 10 minutes or until just crisp-tender. Makes 4 servings.

This was a taste tester favorite. Not as good reheated.

Eggplant Parmesan

1	eggplant, about ¾-pound
½	cup dry white bread crumbs
3	tablespoons grated Parmesan cheese
1	large egg, lightly beaten
½	cup (2-oz) Mozzarella cheese, shredded

Cut eggplant into ¼-inch slices (do not peel).

Combine bread crumbs and Parmesan. Dip eggplant in egg, then in crumb mixture. Place on sprayed baking sheet. Bake 20 to 25 minutes or until lightly browned and cooked through.

Sprinkle cheese on slices and bake just until cheese is melted.

For added color, top with a little marinara or spaghetti sauce.

Sautéed Kale

1	large bunch kale, about 10 ounces
1½	tablespoons oil
	Salt and pepper
2	teaspoons fresh lemon juice

Strip kale leaves from stems. Rinse and drain well.

Heat oil in large nonstick skillet. Add kale and cook covered for 1 minute. Uncover. Cook 1 minute or until just wilted, stirring frequently. Sprinkle lightly with salt, pepper and lemon juice.

There are many reasons to include kale in our diet. It has several disease fighting components and is high in vitamin A, as well as calcium and potassium.

Sautéed Mushrooms

Stove Top

2	tablespoons butter
1	tablespoon oil
8	ounces mushrooms, whole or sliced
½	cup coarsely chopped onion
1	garlic clove, minced

Heat butter and oil in a medium skillet. Add remaining ingredients and cook, stirring frequently, 4 to 5 minutes or until cooked through.

This goes nicely with grilled or broiled steaks.

Grilled Onions

Grill

2	medium onions, sliced 1-inch thick
2	tablespoons butter
	Salt and pepper

Brush onion slices with butter and place on heated grill. Cook until just crisp-tender and lightly browned, turning once. Sprinkle with salt and pepper.

Serve with hamburgers, steaks, pork, or chicken.

Standard Measurements	
Pinch	Less than ⅛ teaspoon
1 tablespoon	3 teaspoons
¼ cup	4 tablespoons
⅓ cup	5 tablespoons + 1 teaspoon
½ cup	8 tablespoons
1 cup	16 tablespoons
2 cups	1 pint
2 pints	1 quart
4 quarts	1 gallon

Grilled Potatoes

If serving the pota-
toes with steaks, cook
and then set aside
to keep hot while
grilling the steaks.

3	large potatoes, peeled
	Salt and pepper
1	onion, sliced
2	cups (8-oz) Cheddar cheese, shredded
½	cup butter, sliced

Slice potatoes into ¼-inch slices. Divide potatoes and place in center of 4 large pieces of heavy-duty foil. Sprinkle with salt and pepper. Top with onion, cheese, and butter.

Tightly fold foil and seal ends. Place on grill and cook 45 to 60 minutes, turning packages several times. Serve in foil. Makes 4 servings.

Oven French Fries

Serve with Flank
Steak, Lemon Broc-
coli and ice cream
topped with straw-
berries for dessert.

2	large baking potatoes
1	tablespoon oil
¼	teaspoon paprika
	Salt

Scrub potatoes, but do not peel. Cut in half lengthwise; cut each half into about 6 wedges.

Place potatoes in a small bowl; sprinkle with oil and paprika. Toss to coat evenly. Arrange potatoes in single layer in a sprayed 11x7-inch baking dish. Bake about 20 minutes, stirring or turning to brown evenly. Cook until tender and lightly browned. Makes 4 servings.

Oven Roasted New Potatoes

Oven 350°F

18	small new red potatoes
¼	cup oil
4	medium garlic cloves, minced
1	tablespoon chopped fresh rosemary

Place potatoes in a large bowl. Add remaining ingredients and toss well to mix.

Spoon into a shallow baking pan and bake 30 to 40 minutes or until potatoes are tender. Makes 6 to 8 servings.

Serve with steaks, chicken or fish.

Scalloped Potatoes Deluxe

Oven 450°F

7	medium potatoes, about 8 cups sliced
2	cups whipping cream
	Salt and pepper
¼	cup freshly grated Parmesan cheese, divided

Peel and slice potatoes about ¼-inch thick. Place half the potatoes in a sprayed 13x9-inch baking dish. Pour half the cream over the potatoes. Sprinkle with salt, pepper, and 2 tablespoons Parmesan cheese. Layer with remaining potatoes, cream, salt, pepper, and cheese. Bake about 45 minutes or until golden and potatoes are tender. Watch closely the last 15 minutes and if too brown, cover with foil. Makes 6 servings.

If desired, you can layer the potatoes with sliced onion, separated into rings. Increase or decrease the cooking time as needed.

This recipe is almost too easy to be so good, but it does come at a price. It is rather expensive to make and high in fat. I usually save it for special occasions. This is also an easy recipe to make for any number of servings. Just layer the dish with the desired amount of potatoes and seasonings. Add cream to almost cover. You shouldn't fill the dish too full or you will have quite a mess in your oven.

Dinner Hash Browns

Microwave
Oven 325°F

Serve these delicious hash browns with Prime rib, pork roast or your favorite chicken recipe.

1   (24-oz) package frozen hash browns, partially thawed
2   cups Half and Half
¼   cup butter
¾   teaspoon salt
⅛   teaspoon white pepper
½   cup grated Asiago cheese

Arrange potatoes in a sprayed 13x9-inch baking dish. Combine half and half, butter, salt, and pepper; heat in microwave or on top of the stove until hot. Pour over potatoes. Sprinkle with the cheese. Bake 40 to 50 minutes or until golden brown. Makes 8 servings.

Garlic Mashed Potatoes

Stove Top

Unless you want a stronger garlic flavor, 1 large garlic clove per pound of potatoes is just about right.

3   pounds potatoes (about 5 medium-large)
3   large garlic cloves, peeled
¼   cup butter
½   cup milk
       Salt and pepper to taste

Peel potatoes; cut each into about 4 pieces. Place in a large pot and cover with water. Add garlic cloves and about a teaspoon salt. Bring to a boil and cook 20 to 30 minutes or until potatoes are tender; drain.

Meanwhile, combine butter and milk and heat until butter is melted (this can be done in the microwave).

Mash potatoes and garlic; add milk mixture, adding just enough to make desired consistency for mashed potatoes (you may not need all of it, depending on the moisture content of the potatoes). Add salt and pepper to taste. Makes about 6 servings.

Au Gratin New Potato Casserole

1¼	cups whipping cream
4	small garlic cloves, peeled, halved
1	pound new red potatoes, unpeeled, thinly sliced
2	tablespoons butter, diced
1½	cups (6-oz) Gruyère cheese

In a medium saucepan, heat the whipping cream and garlic and bring just to a boil. Remove and discard garlic.

Spread the potatoes evenly in a sprayed 11x7-inch baking dish. Pour cream over top. Sprinkle butter over potatoes. Sprinkle with the cheese. Bake 30 to 40 minutes or until potatoes are tender. Cover with foil if cheese is getting too brown. Makes 4 to 6 servings.

Tip: New red potatoes are the very small red potatoes.

Stove Top Oven

I think garlic improves almost any dish, especially this one.

Variation:
Add leftover ham and serve with a green vegetable and tossed salad.

Criss-Cross Potatoes

2	large baking potatoes, halved lengthwise
¼	cup butter, melted
	Salt and pepper
	Paprika

Score potatoes in criss-cross pattern, making cuts about 1-inch deep, without cutting through skins.

Brush with butter. Sprinkle with salt, pepper, and paprika. Place on baking sheet and bake 35 minutes or until tender, basting occasionally with butter. Makes 4 servings.

Oven 450°F

Serve these when you really don't have enough time to cook baked potatoes. A topping isn't really necessary.

Certain cookbook writers turn their noses up at this type of recipe (what, marshmallows!), but our family has enjoyed it every Thanksgiving for three generations. If desired, you can cook fresh sweet potatoes and use in place of the canned.

Stove Top

For such a simple recipe, this version of Rice Pilaf using instant rice has become one of my favorite and most often used recipes.

Candied Sweet Potatoes

Canned sweet potatoes, drained
Butter
Brown sugar
Large marshmallows

Place desired number of sweet potatoes in a shallow baking dish. Top generously with slices of butter. Sprinkle generously with brown sugar and bake 1 hour.

Remove from oven and top with marshmallows spaced 1-inch apart. Return to oven; bake until marshmallows are puffy and lightly browned. Watch carefully.

Almond Rice Pilaf

2	**tablespoons butter**
½	**cup finely chopped onion**
⅓	**cup sliced almonds**
2	**cups chicken broth**
1	**tablespoon chopped fresh parsley or 1 teaspoon dried**
2	**cups uncooked instant rice**

Melt butter in a medium saucepan; add onion and almonds and cook until onion is soft and almonds are just lightly browned. Add broth and parsley and bring to a boil. Stir in rice. Cover; remove from heat and let stand 6 to 7 minutes or until liquid is absorbed. Makes 6 servings.

Family Favorite Rice Dish

1   tablespoon vegetable oil
2   cups instant rice (do not substitute)
1   (2-oz) can sliced mushrooms
1   (10¾-oz) can condensed French onion soup
       Dash of salt and pepper

Heat oil in a small skillet. Add rice and cook until lightly browned, stirring frequently.

Place rice in a sprayed 1½-quart casserole dish. Add remaining ingredients along with ½ *soup can of water*. Bake, covered, 45 to 60 minutes or until liquid is absorbed and rice is tender. Makes 6 servings.

Stove Top
Oven 350°F

Whether being served to family or friends, this flavorful rice dish never fails to please. Our family has enjoyed it for almost forty years. My daughter likes to add water chestnuts, and for a main dish she adds 12 ounces of cooked sausage.

Rice Time Saver

Cook double batches of rice and reheat or use in other favorite dishes. Plain rice will keep up to 1 week in the refrigerator.

Another use is for fried rice. Just add leftover meat, some diced vegetables and then stir-fry. Add a tablespoon of teriyaki or soy sauce for flavor. You now have a one-dish meal with meat and veggies. Add a tossed salad or fruit slices for complete nutrition. Quick - Easy - Delicious

Baked Acorn Squash

Oven 375°F

For easier cutting, poke a few holes in the squash and microwave 3 to 4 minutes before cutting the squash in half.

Acorn squash
Butter
Light brown sugar
Nutmeg

Cut squash in half; remove seeds. Place a generous dab of butter in each cavity. Sprinkle with brown sugar and nutmeg. Place in shallow baking dish; bake 45 minutes or until tender. Makes 2 servings.

Squash & Red Peppers Stir-Fry

Stove Top

Colorful, as well as nutritious.

2	tablespoons oil
½	cup red onion, sliced
1	small red pepper, ¼-inch strips
3	yellow squash, sliced
1	teaspoon dried basil
	Salt and pepper

Heat oil in medium skillet. Cook onion until just tender. Add red pepper and cook until just crisp-tender.

Add squash and basil. Cook until crisp-tender, 4 to 5 minutes, stirring frequently. Add salt and pepper to taste.

Spaghetti Squash

1	spaghetti squash
2	tablespoons butter

Cut squash in half lengthwise. Remove seeds and place, cut-side down, in a shallow pan. Add a small amount of water, about ½ cup, and bake 40 to 50 minutes or until cooked through.

With a fork, pull into strands and toss with just enough butter to lightly coat. Servings depend on the size of the squash.

Oven 350°F

Serve as a substitute for pasta.

Spinach Stir-Fry

3	bunches fresh spinach
4½	tablespoons olive oil
⅓	cup silvered almonds
2	tablespoons soy sauce
1	teaspoon sesame seeds (optional)

Remove stems from spinach, rinse, and spin dry.

Heat oil in a large wok or Dutch oven. Add spinach and cook, stirring frequently, until leaves just start to wilt. This doesn't take long, so don't walk away from it.

Add almonds and soy sauce. Spoon into serving bowl and sprinkle with sesame seeds. Makes about 4 servings.

Stove Top

Don't skimp on the spinach. I am always amazed at how much it cooks down.

Crumb Baked Tomatoes

6	medium tomatoes
2	tablespoons honey
2	slices white bread
1½	teaspoons salt
½	teaspoon pepper
4	teaspoons butter, melted

Remove just the core area from bottom of tomatoes. Turn over and slice off just the top of the tomatoes at the point where you will have a flat surface across. Place in a 13x9-inch baking dish. Drizzle honey over the surface of the tomatoes.

Crumble bread into very small pieces, about ¼-inch. Place in a bowl and combine with the salt, pepper and butter. Sprinkle evenly over the tomatoes.

Bake 10 to 15 minutes or until just heated through. If the bread isn't quite browned enough, place under the broiler until golden. Makes 6 servings.

Oven 350°F

Try to purchase the best-tasting tomatoes you can find. Of course, garden fresh tomatoes are always best.

Zucchini Tomato Casserole

2	medium zucchini, sliced
	Salt and pepper
1	medium onion, thinly sliced
1	green pepper, thinly sliced
2	medium tomatoes, sliced
1½	cups (6-oz) Cheddar cheese, shredded

Place zucchini in a sprayed 2-quart deep casserole dish; sprinkle with salt and pepper.

Top with onions and then the green pepper and tomatoes. Sprinkle with cheese. Bake 50 to 60 minutes. Makes 4 to 6 servings.

Oven 350°F

For crisp vegetables, watch the cooking time carefully. If you prefer the vegetables soft and juicy, cook a few minutes longer.

Index

Great Meals Begin with Six Ingredients Or Less®

Six Ingredients or Less Families on the Go - Our quickest and easiest recipes yet. Designed to get you in and out of the kitchen fast. 288 pages, $16.95.

Six Ingredients or Less Diabetic - Over 400 delicious diabetic conscious, low-fat and low-carb recipes. Includes nutitional analysis and diabetic exchanges. 288 pages, Comb bound, $18.95.

Six Ingredients or Less Low-Carb - Over 600 delicious easy recipes to help you creatively cook with 0 to 6 Net carbs per recipe. Includes nutritional analysis. 288 pages, Comb bound, $18.95.

Six Ingredients or Less - Revised, expanded edition of our best selling all-purpose cookbook. Over 600 delicious recipes from everyday cooking to company entertaining. 352 pages, $16.95.

Six Ingredients or Less Light & Healthy - Devoted to great nutritious cooking that you and your family will enjoy. Nutritional analysis included. 224 pages, $12.95.

Six Ingredients or Less Pasta and Casseroles - Main dish recipes for today's busy lifestyles. An original and low-fat version is given for each recipe. 224 pages, $14.95.

Six Ingredients or Less Slow Cooker - Easy stress-free recipes letting the slow cooker do the work for you. 224 pages, $14.95.

Remember, Cookbooks Make Great Gifts!

sixingredientsorless.com

If you cannot find our cookbooks at your local store, you can order direct.

SIX INGREDIENTS OR LESS
P O BOX 922
Gig Harbor, WA 98335
1-800-423-7184

Families on the Go	(___) # of copies	$16.95 ea	$____
Diabetic Cookbook	(___) # of copies	$18.95 ea (comb bound)	$____
Low-Carb Cooking	(___) # of copies	$18.95 ea (comb bound)	$____
Six Ingredients or Less	(___) # of copies	$16.95 ea	$____
Light & Healthy	(___) # of copies	$12.95 ea	$____
Pasta & Casseroles	(___) # of copies	$14.95 ea	$____
Slow Cooker	(___) # of copies	$14.95 ea	$____

Plus Postage & Handling (First book $3.50, each add'l book, add $1.50) $____

Washington residents add 8.5% sales tax or current tax rate $____

Total $____

Please Print or Type
(Please double-check addition, differences will be billed)

Name_____Phone (__) _____

Address_____

City_____State_____Zip_____

MC or Visa_____ Exp_____

Signature_____